HUSBAND OF ONE WIFE

An Exegesis

Chris Shirley, Jeff Manning,
Mike Trimble, Jeff Blair, Danny Baer

Editor Doug Carey

randall house

114 Bush Rd I Nashville, TN 37217
randallhouse.com

ACKNOWLEDGMENTS

I am incredibly grateful to my fellow Christian pastors and leaders for contributing the vital chapters and viewpoints within this book: Dr. Chris Shirley, Dr. Jeff Manning, Pastor Mike Trimble, Dr. Jeff Blair, and Dr. Danny Baer. These men spent months researching, writing, and praying concerning their respective sections. I am privileged to have such men of godly reputation, character, and ministry experience add their learned voices to such an important topic.

In 2017, a Project Advisory Committee (Mr. Mike Armstrong, Dr. Danny Baer, Dr. Neil Gilliland, Pastor Thomas Hoffmaster, Dr. Jeff Manning, Reverend Mike Wade, Pastor Frank Wiley, Reverend Danny Williams, and Reverend David Williford) was formed to brainstorm and discuss how such a book should be written on such a sensitive topic. This special group of leaders met twice a year in addition to advising me via phone calls, emails, and texts. While the special advisory group met and collaborated, the reader should not assume they approved of everything within this book. However, they all strongly recommended a more detailed discussion about this key passage beyond the view most widely held.

From a ministry perspective, I would be remiss if I did not express appreciation to the three congregations that have called me to shepherd and lead their churches since my return to the ministry in 1994: Crossroads Free Will Baptist (Jenks, Oklahoma), Lowery Free Will Baptist (Twin Oaks, Oklahoma), and First Free Will Baptist (Mobile, Alabama). I am also grateful for the love and grace shown during my first pastorate, ground zero if you would, where this story all began.

Personally, I owe my late parents, Earl and Maudina Carey, who provided an all-important Christian background, environment, and the foundation for spiritual and practical success.

I must also publicly acknowledge my folks, Uncle Wayne and Aunt Lucille McDaniel, who became mine and my brother's legal guardians and gave us a loving, supportive home after our parents' deaths. Even more importantly, they provided a Christian background, environment, and the foundation for spiritual and practical success. It was Uncle Wayne, a dedicated Free Will Baptist pastor for 45 years, who first recognized my leadership potential decades ago and pointed me to Welch College.

Finally, my greatest debt is to my best friend and partner in life, my dear Lorrie Ann, and our two sons. It was in 1992 that we first met in the singles ministry at the Donelson Fellowship. We dated and married after eight months. Through raising two children, three states, four homes, and three churches later, we've been a team. The only regret I have is the same regret all parents share—Christian and Jacob grew up too fast. What I would not give to go back and relive those fun-filled days. Now we also have Christian's wife, Danielle, and our grandchildren, Graham, Nyla, (and one on the way). It's true: grandchildren are special! Lorrie has lived this journey with me and encouraged me to share it. It is to the *Incomparable Lorrie* that I lovingly dedicate this book.

Table of Contents

Prologue

Doug Carey's Story

I will always be indebted to the late Roger Duncan, moderator of the Central Association during my time as pastor in Winter Haven, Florida. Before I left the state to relocate to Nashville, he contacted me and informed me that he had heard my sad news, recognized my innocence, and decided to hold my credentials in "Good Standing." He told me if I ever needed them—which at the time was inconceivable to me—I was to contact him, and he would send them to me.

Books are like life; chapters sometimes take turns you never saw coming. You keep turning pages praying for a good ending. My life story is deeply personal (just like yours), and while I've freely shared many details through the years as a pastor, teacher, and counselor, the true account of what I experienced 31 years ago has *never* been told in any sermon, testimonial, or church conference…much less in a book for friends, acquaintances, and even strangers to digest, until now.

I grew up in a 1960s-70s Christian home, and while our family and extended family, like many families, could be dysfunctional at times, divorce was practically unheard of within our family history. We would hear about celebrity divorces such as Elvis, Elizabeth Taylor, and Sonny and Cher. We would also read about sports figures like Cincinnati catcher Johnny Bench, who announced his divorce—less than one year after he was married. As a huge fan, his divorce truly shocked me. I watched an interview in which he described his first failed marriage: he claimed it just did not work, and that was that. The public did not need to know the details.

Years later, I would come to understand Bench's reluctance to share intensely personal and private details. Even though it has been 30+ years since my own experiences in this area, the memories are often still fresh, and the wounds, though invisible, still occasionally make an emotional appearance. The spouse who has been left behind usually lives with the pain of being abandoned contributing to a small measure of insecurity and failure for many years.

It is not my intention for this book to be solely about me or my story. In no way am I justifying my life's outcome based upon my experience. I sought counsel, insight, and biblical answers regarding 1 Timothy 3:2. I found many people in my own denomination interpreted this verse in more than one way. I too wrestled with it and with God calling me back into the pastorate after my divorce. This book is not about my interpretation of any particular pastoral requirement, but rather an effort to share the various interpretations and help us all gain a clear understanding of Scripture.

So, why revisit the pain endured decades ago? Why describe even a few details of those difficult days that occurred while I was a young pastor? Simply put, to allow God to help pastors, people, and churches who face similar circumstances. The interpretations in this book are not intended to represent the policy of the denomination or local associations. The purpose is to inform, engage, and encourage churches and ordaining councils as they interpret and apply the Scripture.

Neither emotion nor experiences provide truth or values to adopt. Only a correct theological interpretation of Scripture can guide us. This book presents various exegetical views of the biblical passages related to the qualifications of the pastor and explores the phrase the apostle Paul used in 1 Timothy 3:2—*husband of one wife*—not from tradition or preferences but from solid biblical hermeneutics. The scholars will address the different views concerning divorce among pastors. We *must* not shy away from this incredibly difficult and important topic.

CHAPTER ONE

Is the Divorced Minister Permanently Disqualified From Pastoral Ministry?

By Chris Shirley, Ph.D.,
associate dean, Professor of Educational Ministries,
Southwestern Baptist Theological Seminary,
Fort Worth, Texas

I simply could not envision any scenario where a church would be interested in using me in a leadership position, much less actually call me as pastor—divorce, for whatever reason, even a biblical one, wrecked for all time any minister's possible future ministry, not to mention his reputation.—Doug Carey

Introduction

Few would argue that the bedrock institutions of society have suffered unrelenting attack over the course of the last century; these attacks have accelerated within the first quarter of the 21st century. The ground is shifting rapidly underneath structures representing institutional authority: including government, military, law enforcement, school, church, and home. While some of these fluctuations are the natural results of time and generational movement, the changes we are witnessing in the current era represent a dramatic realignment of culture that threatens to rend irreparably the fabric of society.

The survival of a society depends on the well-being of its families; the home is the foundational building block that undergirds and supports all other components of the social order. Among these components, the church and the home have the most interdependent relationship. Churches reflect the spiritual, social, emotional, and even physical health of their families. In the same way, families reflect the overall condition of their church and its members. Both institutions are facing uphill challenges to their ultimate survival; their resilience will impact all other components at every level.

The barometer of family health is the strength of a marriage, particularly a Christian marriage. The union between a man and a woman, grounded in the Word of God and led by the Holy Spirit, is the greatest asset in the Christian home. The marriage relationship influences not only future generations of children and grandchildren, but also future generations of disciples of Jesus Christ through the home and the church. Without strong marriages, families will falter, and churches will suffer.

Divorce is one of the chief weapons the enemy uses to weaken the family and by association, the church. As divorces have surged in society over the last 50 years, the divorce rate among Christian couples has increased commensurately. Even though divorces among born-again Christians trail the numbers at large, the prevalence of divorce in the church is far too high. The church should be a place of frontline defense in the battle for strong marriages: a place where marriage support, teaching, encouragement, modeling, and mentoring are first-priority ministry tools.

Because of the symbiotic relationship between the home and church, the influence of church leaders as they teach God's truth and model His will for families is paramount. In Titus 1:6-7, the apostle Paul focuses on the life and character of an elder—or pastor—as one who is "above reproach, the husband of one wife, and his children are believers and not open to the charge of debauchery or insubordination. For an overseer, as God's steward, must be above reproach." Implied within Paul's description is the importance of the pastor's example to the flock, specifically in the area of marriage and parenting.

The question is not whether pastor/shepherds have a scriptural requirement to lead by example in their relationships at home and in the church; most biblical scholars and church leaders would agree. There is less consensus, however, on the biblical mandate concerning the pastor's marital history or present status. Can a pastor be divorced, either in the present or the past? Does divorce disqualify a man to serve in the role of a pastor, either in the present or the future? Is a pastor with a spouse who has been divorced still qualified to serve the church as an appointed leader?

The answers to these questions typically fall into one of two broad categories. These categories, however, represent two ends of a continuum. On one side of the scale are those who believe divorce always disqualifies someone to lead the church, regardless of any circumstance or justification. Likewise, the one with a spouse who has been divorced would also be excluded from pastoral ministry. On the other side of the scale are those who believe that divorce, for any reason, should never disqualify someone to serve as a pastor. In between these two perspectives, there are various positions based on biblical interpretation, cultural realities, and personal feelings and opinions.

The purpose of this chapter is to discuss the convictions of those who favor a more restrictive viewpoint: divorce, for any reason, disqualifies someone from pastoral leadership. While this perspective aligns with a strict and more conservative interpretation of Scripture, most who hold this position maintain the need to approach each situation with compassion, grace, and redemption.

Divorce in the Old Testament

Any discussion of pastoral leadership and divorce should begin by defining and describing the boundaries in Scripture. The Old Testament introduces the institution of marriage in Genesis 2:18-25, when God created woman as a "helper" to Adam; in turn, Adam describes God's marvelous creation as "bone of my bones and flesh of my flesh," a reference to the binding covenant relationship they shared with one another. In verse 24, Moses comments on God's will for this marriage: "Therefore a man shall leave his father and his mother and hold fast to his wife, and they shall become one flesh." The Hebrew verb for "hold fast" (*dabaq*) describes the act of clinging or cleaving. God intended for man and woman to have an adhesive relationship that was not easily severed. In the New Testament, both Jesus (Matthew 19:4-7) and Paul (Ephesians 5:31) refer to Genesis 2:24 in discussing God's intention for unity and permanence in marriage.

Unfortunately, the consequences of the fall included not only the severing of man's intimate relationship with God, but also the severing of human relationships as well. Divorce was apparently a common occurrence in primeval cultures. The few Ancient Near Eastern documents that are available indicate some sort of divorce process, although most cultures of the day favored the husband's rights over the wife, who had very few choices; divorce and abandonment brought poverty and deprivation to women without social standing or family wealth.

The "certificate of divorce" mentioned in Deuteronomy 24:1-4 is the first Old Testament reference to a legal process for severing the marriage relationship: "He writes her a certificate of divorce and puts it in her hand and sends her out of his house." Although the act of divorce was relatively simple—a personal note dissolving the marriage—the certificate was a legally required document not only to validate the divorce but also affirm the woman's availability for remarriage. Other references to divorce in the Pentateuch describe specific situations in which divorce was, and was not, permitted (Exodus 21:10-11; Deuteronomy 21:10-14; 22:13-19, 28-29). In most cases, the Lord's provisions for divorce protected the woman from harsh and arbitrary treatment by her husband. There is no evidence in any of the divorce commands that God approved of divorce or that it was an acceptable outcome; these laws merely recognized a process to ameliorate—provide the best outcome—to situations that were already occurring.

Not until later in the Old Testament is divorce mentioned both figuratively and literally. In the period of the divided kingdom, God spoke through His prophets to condemn the idolatry of Israel and Judah. God used the marriage of Hosea and his unfaithful wife, Gomer, as an illustration of His deep and forgiving love for Israel. Gomer's unfaithfulness was certainly worthy of divorce by law, but God commanded the prophet to forgive her wickedness and welcome her back into a covenant relationship. In the same way, God offered Israel grace in the midst of her adulterous behavior with other gods. Israel's choice to sever their relationship with God was their choice, not His. In Isaiah 50:1, the royal prophet expressed Yahweh's frustration with Judah's unfaithful choices with a stern warning about Israel's fate: "Thus says the LORD: 'Where is your mother's certificate of divorce, with which I sent her away?'" The prophet Jeremiah used a similar reference to Israel to caution Judah about the eventual result of her unfaithfulness: "She saw that for all the adulteries of that faithless one, Israel, I had sent her away with a decree of divorce" (Jeremiah 1:8a). Some may point to these prophetic declarations as evidence of God's approval or acceptance of divorce. While these passages certainly communicate God's empathy for the pain experienced by the victims of infidelity, in each case God represents the victim of abandonment rather than the initiator of marital dissolution. The "divorce" that occurs between God and Israel was a recognition of the choices made by Israel and the state of their relationship with the Lord.

In one of the most familiar divorce passages in the Old Testament, the prophet Malachi expressed God's perspective on divorce and its painful consequences (Malachi 2:10-16). The KJV translates verse 16 as "For the LORD, the God of Israel, saith that He hateth putting away: for one covereth violence with his garment." However, most modern translations use a similar message from a different viewpoint, as represented here from the ESV: "For the man who does not love his wife but divorces her, says the LORD, the God of Israel, covers his garment with violence." In either case, God's opinion of divorce is stated clearly: divorce is an act born out of sin that does "violence" to a relationship instituted by God.

The only instance in which spiritual leadership and divorce are connected in the Old Testament occurs in Leviticus 21:7. Among the holiness requirements for God's priests is one pertaining to marriage: "They shall not marry a prostitute or a woman who has been defiled, neither shall they marry a woman divorced from her husband, for the priest is holy to his God." As those who led God's people to reflect His holy nature (Leviticus 11:44), the priests were required to live a consecrated life; God expected His servant leaders to exemplify His holiness in every area of life. By implication from this command, one could also assume that priests were also not allowed to be divorced. Although men outside the priesthood were not prohibited from marrying a legally divorced woman, priests who married a divorced woman—or any woman who had been with another man—would be considered ritually unclean and unacceptable for holy service in representing Yahweh to His people.

God's message on divorce in the Old Testament rings clear and consistent.

- Divorce is an aberration of God's design for man and woman to be in a committed and abiding relationship with Him and one another.
- Divorce destroys or does "violence" to a relationship; there are no "victimless" divorces. Ultimately, God is the offended party to every divorce.

- Although God acknowledges the reality of fractured marriages and divorce, and desires to protect its victims, He does not approve of divorce, nor does He recommend or initiate divorce.

- God chooses spiritual leaders to exemplify His character in every aspect of life; divorce, being contrary to God's design, disqualifies a man from leadership in God's holy community.

Divorce in the New Testament

The New Testament message on divorce serves as both commentary and application for the teaching of the Old Testament. Marriage as an abiding covenant relationship under God's command is still upheld as the ideal relationship between man and woman. Divorce is recognized as a cultural reality and legal option. Marital commitment is identified as God's will for all people but identified as a prime qualification for leadership in the family of God.

Matthew opens his gospel with a looming divorce. When Joseph discovered that Mary was "with child from the Holy Spirit...her husband Joseph, being a just man and unwilling to put her to shame, resolved to divorce her quietly" (Matthew 1:18-19). Legal divorces, initiated by both men and women, were available through the Jewish legal system (the certificate of divorce) as well as through Roman law. Joseph and Mary were still in the betrothal stage of marriage, a legally binding engagement period that could be severed only through legal divorce. An overnight visit by an angel convinced Joseph to proceed in marriage with the one who would bear the Son of God who would save the world (Matthew 1:20-25).

Jesus' Sermon on the Mount contains the first New Testament teaching on divorce (Matthew 5:31-32). Here, Jesus affirmed God's design for marriage as an exclusive and lifelong relationship between a man and woman; but at the same time, He acknowledges the reality that sexual infidelity (*porneia*) can irreparably damage the marriage covenant.

At the same time, Jesus does not command or approve of divorce in this or any circumstance. The implication of Jesus' reference to adultery implies that divorce for any other reason is unacceptable and puts all parties in a potentially adulterous situation.

Later in Jesus' ministry (Matthew 19:3-9), some Pharisees called on Jesus to clarify His teaching on divorce by settling an ongoing argument about the meaning of "he has found some indecency in her" from Deuteronomy 24:1. Those who followed Shammai interpreted the qualification—indecency—as a serious moral failing, primarily sexual infidelity. Followers of the teachings of Hillel interpreted the same idea as anything that might diminish a wife in the eyes of her husband. This interpretation came to be known as an "any cause" divorce and was accepted widely in Jewish society. The Pharisees' question was crafted to force Jesus to take a stand on the issue, which would likely alienate Him from one school or the other. While Jesus' answer aligned Him clearly with Shammai's teaching ("except for sexual immorality"), Jesus prefaced His answer with a lesson on the significance of marriage. He appealed to God's original design for marriage in which husband and wife would "hold fast" or cling to one another. Consequently, finding arbitrary reasons for dissolving this relationship was contrary to God's will. Jesus also reminded the Pharisees that God only allowed divorce to protect the victims of divorce from the sinful intentions of a hardhearted spouse (Matthew 19:8).

We find Mark's version of this conversation in Mark 10:2-12. In this synoptic account, Jesus did not mention the exclusion for sexual immorality; Jesus offered no allowance for divorce. Likely, however, the difference between these two accounts is not one of a disagreement but of summarization. In most cases, Mark offers a condensed narrative of the conversations and events in Jesus' life. Similar to Matthew 19, we hear Jesus focus on the sanctity of marriage as the primary issue stemming from the Pharisees' question. Mark's omission of the exclusion was undoubtedly based on his assumption that his readers would understand that sexual infidelity was an understood allowance upon which all parties in the conversation would agree.

Referring back to Jesus' teaching and applying it in a different setting, the apostle Paul addressed specifically the issue of divorce in 1 Corinthians 7:7-12. The broader context of the passage is a part of Paul's answer to questions about the relevance of marriage in light of Jesus' imminent return. He addressed those who were already married, those who were single, and those who might be contemplating divorce. As a general message, Paul admonished all parties to be content in their present state: if married, remain married and thrive in that relationship, if single, remain single (if possible) and dedicate your life to Kingdom ministry. Paul recognized there could be situations in which an unbelieving husband or wife might choose to leave their Christian spouse based on their spiritual incompatibility. In these cases, Paul advised the believers not to hinder the unbelieving spouse from leaving; Roman divorce only required the initiating spouse to leave the home for the dissolution to be effective. The apostle thereby opened an allowance for divorce based on being unequally yoked. Even then, Paul was not offering an approval or acceptance of divorce; he encouraged both husbands and wives of unbelievers to stay married if their partner was willing to remain.

Ultimately, Paul's perspective on divorce was grounded in his theology on marriage. The apostle reiterates God's design for marriage from Genesis 2:24 within his discussion of the church's reflection of family unity in Ephesians 5:22-33: "Therefore a man shall leave his father and mother and hold fast to his wife, and the two shall become one flesh." Paul likened the mystery of the unity of the marriage relationship to the unity the church experiences in Christ. Holding fast or cleaving in marriage represents a spiritual unity that should not be undone but should be cherished and maintained in a lifelong, committed relationship.

God's message on divorce in the New Testament is consistent with Old Testament teaching, and in some cases, speaks of a higher standard for marriage.

- Christian marriage has a spiritual dimension of unity and permanence akin to one's relationship with Christ and the body of Christ.

- Divorce is contrary to God's design for marriage.

- Believers should seek every opportunity to maintain and sustain their marriage relationship and exemplify the forgiveness and grace of God through Christ.

The Old Testament on Leadership

God always considered Himself to be the model leader of His people. The Pentateuch places God front and center as the leader of Abraham and his descendants. God chose Abraham to initiate His plan for the redemption and blessing the world. God orchestrated the events that eventually led to the formation of a nation bearing His name. He set the standards for worship and established the laws by which His people would live. He rewarded their obedience and punished their rebellion. Above all, God loved His children, saved them from their sinful choices, and "held fast" to those who followed Him.

Even though God is continually described in Scripture as the sovereign leader of His people, He nonetheless worked through human leaders to accomplish His will. He worked through Moses, Aaron, Joshua, and numerous judges to form, establish, and maintain a ragtag confederation of tribes into a national power. God used prophets, priests, Levites, and others to keep the people focused on worship and fidelity to the one true God, the Great I Am. God established kings, queens, and a multitude of royal leaders and ruled over them as they succeeded and failed in their efforts to follow God's lead in moving Israel toward its ultimate destiny.

The story of Israel and its leaders provides a deeper look into the nature of spiritual leadership and God's expectations for those who join Him in leading His people.

Leading God's people begins in the home. In Genesis 18:19, the Lord describes Abraham's first leadership responsibility: "For I have chosen him, that he may command his children and his household after him to keep the way of the LORD by doing righteousness and justice, so that the LORD may bring to Abraham what he has promised him." Unlike modern secular leaders, whose family situation and background are increasingly irrelevant to their qualification for leadership, God has always placed a premium on one's ability to lead at home. Even celebrated biblical leaders like David and Solomon were diminished by their inability to lead at home and provide a godly example in marriage.

God's leaders are called to ministry. God called Moses with a voice from a burning bush and appointed him to ministry leadership: "Come, I will send you to Pharaoh that you may bring my people, the children of Israel, out of Egypt" (Exodus 3:10). God used Moses to rescue His people from bondage in Egypt and move them to the Promised Land. Moses did not ask for nor seek this role; God, in His wisdom, chose Moses and empowered him to accomplish what man could not do alone. One's call to Christian leadership is a holy appointment with high standards and expectations; Moses' lack of trust in God at Kadesh, when he impulsively struck the rock for water (Numbers 20:10-12), disqualified both he and Aaron from entering the Promised Land.

God's leaders are blameless. Blameless does not mean perfect or sinless, neither of which is possible for any person. Being blameless connotes a reputation of unquestionable integrity. In the case of God's leaders, blameless living provides no room for attack from enemies seeking to smear the reputation or intentions of a Christian leader. Blameless leaders are trusted because their words and actions are a testimony to their faith. In his final address to Israel, the prophet Samuel stood before the people and declared his blamelessness: "…I have walked before you from my youth until this day. Here I am; testify against me before the LORD and before his anointed. Whose ox have I taken? Or whose donkey have I taken? Or whom have I defrauded? Whom have I oppressed? Or from whose hand have I taken a bribe to blind my eyes with it?" (1 Samuel 12:2-3). Samuel's confrontation with Israel was not an attempt to aggrandize himself but to emphasize the importance of blameless leadership. Their desire for an earthly king—leading to the appointment of Saul—would highlight the disastrous results of following a leader with a questionable reputation.

God's leaders have a true love for the Lord. No other leader in the Old Testament exemplifies this characteristic to a greater degree than David. Samuel described David as "a man after [God's] own heart" (1 Samuel 13:14), indicating an intimate relationship between Yahweh and the man He had chosen to lead Israel. David demonstrated his love for God through words and actions. The psalms are replete with David's expressions of love and worship for the God upon whom he depended. One of the ways David desired to prove his love to God was to build a temple to His honor. God, however, did not allow David to fulfill his dream: "You have shed much blood and have waged great wars. You shall not build a house to my name, because you have shed so much blood before me on the earth" (1 Chronicles 22:8). David's background in warfare disqualified him from building the temple; God's plan was to have a man of peace (Solomon) construct a house of worship for the Lord.

God's leaders seek wisdom. Solomon, of course, is the biblical archetype of a wise leader (at least in the opening years of his reign). When God came to Solomon with an open hand ("Ask what I shall give you"), the king asked for "an understanding mind to govern your people, that I may discern between good and evil, for who is able to govern this your great people?" (1 Kings 3:5, 9). Solomon used his wisdom to guide Israel to become one of the strongest and most prosperous nations in the region. Unfortunately, Solomon made unwise choices—like his father, David—in not applying God's wisdom to family leadership. When the throne passed to the next generations, Solomon's son was not prepared to hold together the kingdom.

God's leaders speak truth. From the moment God called him to a prophetic ministry, Jeremiah struggled with the immense challenge of going to the religious establishment in Judah with a confrontational message from God: "Ah, LORD God! Behold, I do not know how to speak, for I am only a youth" (Jeremiah 1:6). Despite Jeremiah's protestations, the Lord promised him, "Do not be afraid of them, for I am with you to deliver you" (Jeremiah 1:8). Jeremiah accomplished God's plan and delivered a difficult message to hardhearted people. The prophet called Israel to discard their adulterous ways and return to the One who loved them first and most. He spoke the truth, even in the face of persecution and personal loss. God's leaders are commissioned to speak truth without reservation, and yet with love.

The New Testament on Leadership

No discussion about the essentials of Christian leadership would be complete without acknowledging the Master Leader, Jesus Christ. In Him, we see the perfect representation of God's leadership over His people and the clearest example for human leaders to follow. All principles of leadership gleaned from the Old Testament are applicable in the New Testament; these principles, however, are now incarnated in the Son. As God the Father established Himself as the model leader for Israel in the Old Testament, so we see God the Son claim the same role over the community of faith—the church—in the New Testament: "And he is the head of the body, the church. He is the beginning, the firstborn from the dead, that in everything he might be preeminent" (Colossians 1:18). Those Christ chooses and calls to be leaders in the church should follow in His footsteps.

God's leaders are shepherds. In John 10, Jesus used the image of a shepherd to describe His leadership role. This illustration would have been a familiar allusion to His disciples; their Scripture contained numerous references to the spiritual leader as a shepherd (e.g., Numbers 27:17; Jeremiah 3:15; Zechariah 10:2). Jesus, however, set Himself apart as the "good shepherd" in contrast to the "hired hand" (John 10:12-13), who has no relationship with or ultimate concern for the sheep. Jesus' shepherd goes before the flock (10:4), guides them to rich pastureland (10:9), protects them from danger (10:10), cares for each of His sheep with intimate concern, and sacrifices His own well-being for the sake of the sheep (10:15). The apostles understood their role as a pastor-shepherd in the image of Jesus. In Peter's first epistle, the apostle instructs elders or overseers, i.e., pastors, to take their cues from "the chief Shepherd" and lead the people with humility and honor, striving to be "examples to the flock" (1 Peter 5:2-4). The prime example, of course, being Christ Himself.

God's leaders are exemplars. Twice in his epistles, the apostle Paul lists the essential qualifications for church leaders. In 1 Timothy 3:1-13, Paul described the characteristics of the overseer (*episkopos*) and the deacon (*diankonos*), the two offices of the church. Although some of the characteristics appear in both lists, and some are listed under one office or the other, one can assume that most, if not all, of these characteristics would apply to both groups. These qualities apply to one's leadership at home and in marriage ("husband of one wife," "manage his own household well"), in the church ("able to teach," "not a recent convert"), in the community ("respectable," "hospitable,"), and over himself ("self-controlled," "not a drunkard," "not violent...not quarrelsome, not a lover of money"). There could certainly be a longer list of characteristics, but ticking the list was not Paul's intention. Three phrases in this passage—occurring at the beginning, middle, and end—focus on the most important and overriding qualification for leaders: to be "above reproach" (3:2), "well thought of by outsiders" (3:7), "blameless" (3:10), and have a "good standing for themselves" (3:13). In each of these phrases we find the ultimate qualification for leaders: to be an example of Christ-like living at home, in the church, and in the community. This overarching test of leadership is more challenging than simply checking off Paul's list. Paul's discussion of qualifications for elders (*presbuteros*) in Titus 1:5-9 begins, similar to 1 Timothy 3, with the phrase "above reproach" (1:6). Once again, the apostle focuses on the elder or overseer as a model for other believers in his marriage, as a parent, as a teacher and leader in the church, and as a respectable and righteous example of Christ in the community.

Christian Leaders and Divorce

The test for pastoral leadership is multifaceted, and to base one's qualification for ministry on a single issue—like divorce—in isolation from other concerns would be unreasonable. However, a potential leader's marital history and example should be considered among his qualifications, and—arguably—rank among the top tier of considerations. Scripture, both Old and New Testaments, highlights the sacred nature of marriage and the correlation of marriage to spiritual health and fruitfulness. At the same time, the scriptural principles of leadership and God's expectations for leaders should be applied to the fitness of any candidate for a leadership role, especially for those who seek to oversee the body of Christ. The previous sections of this chapter, examining biblical passages concerning marriage, divorce, and spiritual leadership, laid the foundation for the present question: does divorce disqualify a pastor from ministry leadership in the church?

Various Positions

As mentioned earlier in this chapter, there are two ultimate positions to the question of whether a divorce disqualifies a pastor from present and future ministry: yes and no. These two answers, however, are on opposite ends of a spectrum of positions that fall at each end and everywhere in between. The far end of the "no, it does not disqualify" side of the spectrum could be labeled as the *permissive* position: suggesting there are no reasons at any time that divorce would be a disqualifier. Gradually moving toward the center and into the other side of the spectrum, there are a number of *conditional* positions: including pastors who were abandoned by their spouse, pastors who did not initiate a

divorce and attempted to reconcile, or pastors whose spouse was unfaithful and unrepentant. Also included in this group would be pastors
who experienced divorce but chose to remain unmarried because of
their convictions on scriptural teaching. In each of these cases, there
are those who see an allowance in Scripture—either through direct instruction, context considerations, or silence—to sanction pastors who
have experienced divorce or whose spouse has been divorced. On the
"yes, it does disqualify" end of the spectrum are those who believe that
divorce prohibits a man from holding a position of pastoral leadership
in the church. Granted, this *restrictive* position is held by a minority of
people among theologically conservative groups; however, those who
represent this traditional viewpoint believe their case carries a stronger
biblical argument.

The Restrictive Position

The Direct Message from Scripture. Those who hold the restrictive
position on divorce and pastor qualification see a consistent message
throughout Scripture about the permanence of marriage and God's condemnation of divorce. In Genesis 2:24, man and woman are commanded to "hold fast" to one another in marriage: this scriptural expectation
is echoed by the apostle Paul (Ephesians 5:31) and by Jesus (Matthew
19:5-6), who adds a comment on God's exclusive authority in marriage:
"What therefore God has joined together, let not man separate." Even
though divorce was allowed from the early days of Israel's history, God
only permitted divorce to protect innocent victims (Matthew 19:8); the
Lord's disdain for the destructive nature of divorce is evident in Scripture (Leviticus 21:7; Malachi 2:16; Matthew 5:31-32; Mark 10:11-12).

In addition, according to the restrictive position, the apostle Paul's
qualification for church elders and overseers in 1 Timothy 3 and Titus
1 calls for these leaders to be the "husband of one wife." There are
a number of interpretations for this phrase, but the more traditionally
conservative position has been in reference to divorce: one wife for a

lifetime, excluding the death of a spouse. The pastor's marital history and family leadership should be held to the highest standard.

The Indirect Message from Scripture. As stated earlier, in 1 Timothy 3 and Titus 1, Paul's instructions for choosing leaders include several references to the man's overall character and standing in the community, summed up in the phrases "blameless" or "above reproach." These ideas go beyond simple adherence to rules and regulations at a specific point in time. Politicians and other highly visible leaders understand the challenge of being scrutinized for a lifetime of words and actions, particularly at an earlier and less mature season of life. Apologies and explanations do not always remove lingering questions people have about their current fitness for leadership. Those who abide by the restrictive position on divorce believe the questions that may never be fully answered about situations surrounding the divorce can leave hanging questions regarding the pastor's character, leaving him open to reproach within the church and in the wider community. The shepherd is an example to the flock, and his life should reflect a full commitment to Christ and his family in every season, as a model for others to follow.

The Need for Grace. The restrictive perspective is not a graceless position. Those who believe divorce disqualifies men from pastoral leadership do not see the same restriction for other ministry opportunities. Everyone in Christ is called to ministry service using the gifts supplied by the Spirit. Pastoral gifts can still be used in a variety of ministries outside the role of an appointed shepherd or lead pastor. While the past and its natural consequences cannot be erased, repentance brings full forgiveness from the Lord. Finding those opportunities in another venue of ministry can provide those with pastoral gifts the potential to grow in their faith and still be fruitful in God's kingdom work.

CHAPTER TWO

Must the Local Church Pastor Be Married?

By Jeff Manning, D.Min.,
pastor, Unity Free Will Baptist Church,
Greenville, North Carolina

> *To prevent ministers from making the same mistake I did*
> *many years ago, we need to guide our aspiring pastors (and*
> *those whose wife has passed away) from thinking they must*
> *be married to do ministry.—Doug Carey*

Prerequisite. A prerequisite is something that is required as a prior condition before something else can happen. In the realm of education, a "prerequisite" is a course or some other requirement that must be fulfilled before enrolling in a particular course or program. Ten years into pastoral ministry at the church I still pastor, three different people within a 10-day period asked me, "Jeff, have you thought about furthering your education?" Ironically (or providentially!), I had. Consequently, I scoured the Internet looking for seminaries offering the degree I was most interested in—a Doctor of Ministry Degree (D.Min.) in expository preaching. The schools offering such a degree required prerequisites. For example, I had to have a Master of Divinity (M.Div.) degree, or its equivalent, and a minimum of three years of significant post-M. Div. ministry experience. I met the prerequisites. I enrolled at Southern

Seminary in Louisville, Kentucky, and graduated with my D.Min. degree in 2002.

Stipulations Versus Expectations

Similarly, there are prerequisites that must be fulfilled before a man can assume the position of a local church pastor. Paul tells Timothy, for example, that a pastor must be "blameless" and "able to teach," and he must not be "quarrelsome" or "covetous" (1 Timothy 3:2-3). But what about his marital status? Is marriage a pastoral prerequisite? Must a preacher of the gospel commit himself in holy matrimony to a wife before he can commit himself to pastoral ministry to a church? Some would say, "Absolutely, he must be married, because Paul states in 1 Timothy 3:2a that he *must* be 'the husband of one wife.'" But did Paul mean a man *had* to be married? Is marriage truly a prerequisite for a local church pastor? Must a man be a "husband" before he can be a "pastor"? We will walk through the whole counsel of Scripture in seeking an answer to that question.

Expectation or Stipulation

An *expectation* is a belief or anticipation of something that is likely to happen, while a *stipulation* is a condition or requirement that is mandatory before an agreement can be reached.

This *expectation* versus *stipulation* debate took center stage in our church several years ago. Our student minister resigned to teach youth and family ministry courses at Welch College. Our church began the search and interviewed Jake, a young graduate with a degree in pastoral ministry. However, *he was not married*. In fact, in the days leading up to one of his interviews with our search committee, he and his fiancé broke up. We had hired our former youth pastor as a single man just over two years earlier, but he was engaged to get married four months after we hired him. With this candidate, marriage was now off the table for the foreseeable future. How would the search committee respond to this? How would the church family respond to this? Did they have an *expectation* of hiring a pastoral staff member who was married? I'm sure most of them did. But did they view marriage as a necessary *stipulation* before pastoral duties can be fulfilled? Evidently not, because he was eventually hired with an over ninety percent vote. But the Lord was so very kind and gracious to him and our church. Jake's ministry as a single student pastor flourished, and it wasn't too long before the Lord brought a young lady into his life. We marveled and praised God for his providence in all of this.

Of all the stipulations/expectations for a pastor, this one concerning his marriage is certainly the most hotly debated. Chapters one (Shirley) and five (Baer) of this book deal with whether he can continue in pastoral ministry after his marriage is dissolved through divorce. Chapter three (Trimble) examines the question of whether all the qualifications carry equal weight. Chapter four (Blair) addresses the question of polygamy and whether that was Paul's concern when detailing the qualifications for pastoral candidates in 1 Timothy 3 and Titus 1. But this chapter will focus on whether marriage itself is mandated or simply expected, basically whether being single prohibits someone from pastoral ministry. That marriage is *expected* is further developed in 1 Timothy 3:4 where the pastoral candidate is required to rule his household (not just himself) well, and to have his children in biblical submission to his fatherly authority. The implication is spelled out in verse five: "For if a man know not how to rule his own house, how shall he take care of the church of God?" (KJV). This is certainly understandable. Since the church is likened unto a household—God's household—why would a church think a man would manage it well if his track record with his own family was a colossal failure? If a man cannot properly manage his children, why should a church think he will be able to effectively manage "God's children"? Failure at home does not bode well for success at the church. If a man cannot properly manage things on a small scale "under his own roof," it is predictable that he will not manage things well "under the church's roof." If his household is in shambles, then so is his credibility. Paul echoes this same sentiment to Titus, when he instructed him to appoint pastors in every town, and then provided the criteria for such appointments:

> If anyone is above reproach, the husband of one wife, and his children are believers and not open to the charge of debauchery or insubordination. [7] For an overseer, as God's steward, must be above reproach. He must not be arrogant or quick-tempered or a drunkard or violent or greedy for gain, [8] but hospitable, a lover of good, self-controlled, upright, holy, and disciplined. [9] He must hold firm to the trustworthy word as taught, so that he may be able to give instruction in sound doctrine and also to rebuke those who contradict it (Titus 1:6-9).

Untenable Conclusions of the Marriage Mandate

If Paul instructs that a pastor is to be a husband and manage his household well, then logically both marriage and children are required based on the same argument. While marriage is clearly *anticipated* by anyone pursuing the office of a pastor, if we go a step further and make marriage a *stipulation*—an unwavering mandate—then some troubling and even absurd conclusions arise. First, Paul himself was not qualified (1 Corinthians 7:7-8), and neither was Jesus! If marriage is an absolute prerequisite for a minister, then Jesus was not qualified to pastor a local church. And while anecdotal, it is interesting to note how the early church was predominantly led by single men—e.g., Paul, Luke, Silas, Barnabas, Timothy, Titus, etc.

Second, if the pastoral candidate "*must* be a husband" (1 Timothy 3:2), then, to be consistent, he must also be required to have more than one child. Why? Because in 1 Timothy 3:4 and Titus 1:6 Paul uses the plural "children." Therefore, unless and until a man has at least two children, he is not qualified for pastoral ministry. *Really?* Can you imagine churches advertising their need of a pastor and stipulating that the only candidates who will be considered are those with two or more children?

Third, if marriage is a non-negotiable *stipulation*, then what happens to the pastor whose wife precedes him in death? Is that pastor suddenly disqualified from pastoral ministry? Imagine this scenario: your wife dies on a Tuesday, you have the funeral visitation that Friday, the funeral on Saturday, and then you resign from your church on Sunday. As crazy as that sounds, it is technically what would be expected if a church demands its pastors be a *husband.* And we will not even go to the absurdity of what would happen to a pastor if one of his two children died leaving him with only one child to manage.

A church simply has no biblical authority to mandate a pastor be married. Yes, the implications of Scripture and the expectations of congregations show that, in the majority of cases, he will be married to a godly wife and have children that are well-behaved and hopefully, if they are old enough, following Christ as their Savior and Lord. But to disqualify a man because of his singleness—or his only having one child—is to "raise the bar" to an unbiblical level.

It may be helpful to think of it in an "if then" context, as Scripture does in other places (e.g., 2 Corinthians 5:17, "If anyone is in Christ, [then] he is a new creation"). Therefore, "IF" he is married, then he must be "the husband of one wife" (or a "one-woman man"), someone who is totally devoted to his wife, someone who seeks to love his wife like Christ loves His church (Ephesians 5:25). And "IF" he has children still living at home and subject to his parental authority, then he must be leading them in such a way to demonstrate his capability, with the Lord's help, to effectively lead a local body of believers. And for clarity, there is no condition regarding his morality in general or his sexual purity in particular. He *must* be a moral man and sexually pure whether or not he is married. He must also be able to teach and not covetous, regardless of his marital status.

BUT...

But what about all the disadvantages of a single man serving as a pastor? And what about the dangers of a man serving without a wife by his side? Actually, Paul contends there are significant *advantages* of singleness and celibacy.

> Now as a concession, not a command, I say this. [7] I wish that all were as I myself am. But each has his own gift from God, one of one kind and one of another.... [32] I want you to be free from anxieties. The unmarried man is anxious about the things of the Lord, how to please the Lord. [33] But the married man is anxious about worldly things, how to please his wife, [34] and his interests are divided. And the unmarried or betrothed woman is anxious about the things of the Lord, how to be holy in body and spirit. But the married woman is anxious about worldly things, how to please her husband (1 Corinthians 7:6-7, 32-34).

Paul, as a single (or single-again) man, while realizing that many are not "called to singleness," nonetheless wishes that more were single so more devotion could be given to the advancement of God's kingdom (verse 7). An unmarried man, whose heart is set on Christ and has pledged his ultimate allegiance to Him, can spend more time doing the Lord's work and thinking about various ways to serve Him and His church. A married man, who has the same passion for Christ, cannot possibly spend as much undivided time and energy serving the Lord and His church for the simple fact that he has responsibilities at home to his wife (and children)—responsibilities that are also Bible-based and righteous (and if he does not meet those responsibilities, he is disqualified as a pastor for not having his household in order!). In other words, Paul is not arguing that singleness is right or better than marriage. He is simply stating that marital status does affect a person's life and ministry.

A pastor with a wife and children will not be able to devote as many hours to his ministry as a single pastor, without doing harm to his role as a husband and father. While a married minister needs to spend quality time with his family—dating his wife, watching the kids so his wife can catch her breath and maintain her sanity, attending his kids' ballgames and recitals, playing with them, and discipling them, etc.—the single minister could spend all that time edifying the body of Christ in numerous ways. If Paul had been a married man after his conversion, the whole Book of Acts would read differently. To faithfully fulfill his duties at home, Paul could not possibly have planted as many churches and evangelized as many cities as he did as a single man. His singleness afforded him some advantages that a married minister could not have experienced. And the same is true of single pastors today. The fewer the distractions, the greater the devotion. The less time and energy needed at home, the more time and energy available for ministry—for preparing sermons, discipling people, hosting small groups, attending committee meetings, serving on boards, ministering to shut-ins, counseling, etc.

This discrepancy in time and energy is well noted by Billy Graham in a letter to his friend John Stott who was a lifelong single. He wrote, "Thank you for your November letter. Just reading it made me a bit exhausted! How do you do it my friend? If you had a wife, five children, five in-laws—and 15 grandchildren, it would be rather difficult. Please forgive me if I am not able to keep up with you!"

Steve DeWitt is senior pastor of Bethel Church in Northwest Indiana. He served as a single pastor for 19 years—14 of them as a lead pastor. On his 10th anniversary at Bethel, the church organized a time of celebration. One of the points emphasized during the festivities was the blessing Steve's singleness had been, affording him time and energy to be invested in the church that a married pastor could not match. One faithful member told him, "I selfishly hope you stay single so you can stay focused on us."[1] Sounds like that member was familiar with Paul's first letter to the Corinthians!

Advantages and Disadvantages: A Two-Way Street

While there are clearly some practical advantages of a minister being single, as mentioned above, there are also some perceived disadvantages of being a single pastor. *How will a single man be able to relate to those who are married, and what about those who are married with a quiver full of children? How will he effectively minister to the women since he does not have a wife? How can a single man possibly have a healthy and balanced ministry?*

Obviously, there are numerous benefits of a minister being married to a godly woman. To name only a few, God can use her to help shape and mold her husband's character and personal holiness. She can lovingly point out his blind spots and his unrealized episodes of selfishness. She can serve the church family alongside her husband and be a tremendous blessing to the women. She can help her husband better minister to the opposite sex. Together, they can help each other establish credibility and maturity and develop more and more Christlikeness. A godly wife helps her husband avoid sexual temptations (1 Corinthians 7:1-5), and she can provide a female perspective on church-related issues.

Regarding a single pastor's ability to relate to those who are married or to families with children, while there are numerous advantages of being married and building credibility by raising a godly family, those must not be perceived as essentials before a man of God can effectively teach and preach the Scriptures. After all, what is more important and powerful, one's ability to relate experientially or one's ability to exegete and expound and apply the Scripture to people's lives? What's more important, human experience or divine wisdom? If you argue that experience is critical and an unmarried, experiential novice cannot possibly have a healthy, balanced, and fruitful ministry, you will argue yourself into a very uncomfortable corner. Jesus and Paul, as single men, both taught effectively on marriage and the family. Experience and role-modeling should not, in fact, they *cannot* be expected in all situations. It is simply not possible and not supported by Scripture. I have never been physically handicapped, yet I have the privilege of ministering to several special-needs individuals in my church. I have never been a woman or a black man or an Indian, and yet, with the Lord's help, I teach and preach the Word to all three categories of people every Sunday. I have never been a millionaire or a medical doctor, and yet I also have those types of people in my church. Just as experiential role-modeling is not required in these cases for me to effectively minister to these people, so marriage and fatherhood are not required before a man can be used of the Lord to minister to families.

Churches having an *expectation* of its pastors being married and having adorable kids is not unreasonable—and the majority of pastors will. If, however, a church stipulates that a pastor *must* be a married man, then it takes a position that is unbiblical and essentially puts words in God's mouth, making the requirements of a minister more restrictive than the Lord intended them to be. If God does not *require* a pastor be a married man, then neither should a pulpit committee or a church congregation.

Endnotes

[1] DeWitt, Steve. (2011, March 26). "That's Odd": On Bias Against Single Pastors. Retrieved June 17, 2020, from https://www.thegospelcoalition.org/article/thats-odd-on-bias-against-single-pastors/.

CHAPTER THREE

Is "Husband of One Wife" More Important Than the Other Pastoral Qualifications or Do They Possess Equal Weight?

By Mike Trimble, M.Div.,
pastor, Kirby Free Will Baptist Church,
Kirby, Michigan

People find it both amazing and confusing when pastors occasionally excuse their weaknesses concerning other pastoral requirements, while holding one requirement to a higher standard on that same list.—Doug Carey

The calls routinely come in. "Our pastor is leaving us. Do you know *anybody* who is available?" My response is typical, "What are you looking for?" It is here they launch into their *wish* list: Is he good with old people? Can he reach young people while working with the backbone of the church? Can he preach, teach, win the lost, disciple the saints… and it would be a great blessing if his wife could play the piano! (Their list is usually comprised of essential abilities to address the current issues, problems, or crisis that exist in their church.) Of course, there's always one more requirement: *he must not be divorced, period.*

Based on the criteria of their list, a potential pastor is chosen to "candidate" before the church. The candidate comes with a family in tow to be interviewed by the church, and vice versa. At this juncture, it becomes obvious most of the people in the church have their own *wish list.* It is personal and usually driven by the needs of their family and their preferences. And it usually is revealed in a form of rhetorical questions that if answered correctly by the pastoral candidate results in that family being able to check the "yes" box: *Is he a good communicator? Can he relate well to my kids? Will he be able to bring new people in? How will he get rid of the people keeping the new people from attending and staying in church? Will he change anything I like? Is he personable? Is he a good guy? Does he have kids who will become friends with my kids? Will his sermons inspire me? Will he be the pastor my family and I need?* (Needless to say, almost everyone in the church possesses a list, whether it is articulated or not.)

Thankfully, there are lists of inspired pastoral qualifications found in the Bible. These lists were given by the Apostle Paul to his young "sons" in the ministry, Timothy and Titus, who were his special liaisons for handling important assignments in the church. The lists of pastoral qualifications are found in 1 Timothy 3:1-7 and Titus 1:5-9. Another direct reference to pastoral character is given in broad strokes and can be found in 1 Peter 5:1-4. Combined, these passages give a minimum of 20 specific qualifications for the pastor/shepherd of the church. However, there is one qualification that appears to have risen to the top spot. For many, violate this one stipulation and present and future pastoral ministry is over. Transgress most of the other qualifications and there is little to no repercussion.

1 Timothy List

The 1 Timothy list will be better understood with a little background information. The Apostle Paul wrote the epistle as a personal letter to Timothy (while he was serving in Ephesus as Paul's special representative) to specifically address certain problems and issues (1 Timothy 1:3-7). Paul's primary concerns can be categorized under two headings: doctrine specific soteriology (1:5; 2:8-15; 3:1-16; 4:6-16; 5:4-6, 8; 6:3-5, 11-14, 18-19) and ecclesiology, dealing with the two key positions in the church (2:1-15; 3:1-13; 4:6-16; 5:1-6). Timothy was competent to help address these issues. Paul and Timothy met during Paul's second missionary journey in Timothy's hometown of Lystra (Acts 16:1-5). He was impressed with Timothy's spiritual heritage (2 Timothy 1:5) and maturity. He was invited to travel with Paul and Silas to spread the gospel, establish churches and be mentored by the apostle as they traveled together. Their close relationship was marked by Paul's declaration of Timothy as his "son in the faith" (1 Timothy 1:2). They were united in Christ, committed to the church, and were stalwart defenders of the faith.

Paul had served as pastor in Ephesus for three years (52-55 AD). Ephesus was a thoroughly Greek-influenced city in the province of Asia Minor. One would imagine with Pastor Paul at the helm there would be no problems in the church, but this was not the case. The church was relatively young, perhaps about ten years old, with a leadership issue. In the absence of a strong pastor there were doctrinal deviations, myth musings, devotions to endless genealogies, and dead-end discussions. There was a lack of commitment to basic biblical truths, which promoted swerving from sound doctrine and wandering from the purposes of the church. The lack of mature, sound believers willing to lead and speak allowed the immature, uninformed, and false teachers to speak as if they possessed understanding, thus bringing confusion into the church. Timothy was tasked by Paul to address these problems primarily by putting the right kind of leaders in place (1 Timothy 1:3-7).

Paul's "playbook" began with recruiting qualified leaders for two key positions: pastor and deacon. As previously noted, Paul's list of qualifications for pastors is found in 1 Timothy 3:1-7 with a parallel list in Titus 1:5-9. Some Bible scholars believe the list to be reflective of a template of other qualifications and lists for various occupations of the day.[1] Other scholars oppose this position. It seems reasonable to assume Paul may have used an existing template model while adapting the wording specifically for the context of the Ephesian church under the inspiration of the Holy Spirit. The point to understand is, whether for secular or sacred purposes, there were expectations in the Roman world for certain basic qualifications to be met for those in key leadership positions.

Paul certainly had qualifications in mind for the key leaders in the church. A question to consider is, were these church leadership lists exhaustive? There are other places in the Bible where qualifications for church leadership are mentioned. The first church leadership list can be found in Acts 6:1-7, which describes qualifications of seven men who would assist the apostles in Jerusalem. These men certainly could be considered forerunners for the office of deacon. Paul would have been familiar with this list. A simple reading of both lists demonstrates that while there are no contradictions, there are differences in scope. For example, the list in Titus excludes the qualification of "not being a recent convert" found in 1 Timothy. Perhaps it was because the Ephesian Church was an established church of at least ten years while the church in Crete was so new almost everyone within the congregation would have been considered a new convert.

Another difference in Paul's lists is curious: the final qualification in 1 Timothy, "well thought of by outsiders" is omitted in the Titus list, even though evangelical churches would agree on its importance. A plausible explanation is that Cretan culture did not honor, value, or recognize the values of the Christian faith. Clearly, the Ephesus and Crete churches existed at the same period but the different cultures account for the differences in the lists. This explanation does no harm to the Scriptures or to the integrity of the office of overseer.

The 1 Timothy 3 List Examined

Paul began with a statement intended to elevate the calling and ministry of the overseer. The word *bishop* (in some translations) is used interchangeably with overseer, with each supporting the premise that the position included oversight of the church. Paul was not requesting that Timothy begin a new office in the church. Men were already functioning in the position (Acts 14:23; 20:17, 28). Paul's intent was to bring some degree of structure and a basic threshold of qualifications for overseers who were to help lead the church. Using a modern metaphor, Paul was trying to get the right people on the right bus and in the right seats on the bus.

The phrase "this saying is trustworthy" (*pistos ho logos*) is a familiar and important phrase Paul used to indicate the importance of what precedes or follows it. This phrase signals the significance of the office and qualifications of the pastor/overseer. It also commends the pastorate as a noble endeavor worthy of consideration.

Verse 2 lists seven qualifications. The first is "above reproach." The Greek word for reproach (*anepilempton*) can be translated "irreproachable, blameless, perfect, not open to attack or criticism." Using words such as "blameless" or "perfect" leave no margin for error. The fact is, no one knows of a perfect pastor or a blameless overseer. They simply do not exist. The idea, which is a consistent theme throughout Paul's list, is the pastor should be faithful. Specifically, in this phrase, his devotion and faithfulness to God should be well known to others.

The next qualification is not the centerpiece of Paul's list, but it is the focal point of our discussion. The style of Paul's list is short, staccato-like phrases with little elaboration. One can assume the Greek words used were well known and self-explanatory to the intended audience of his day.

In the English Bible, the qualification typically reads "husband of one wife." In the Greek, this is a three-word phrase. It reads *mias gynaikos andra,* which translates literally "one woman man." Paul writes nothing more, nothing less. He simply states it and moves on. We will move on as well; however, we will return to this issue at the conclusion of this list.

The next four qualifications are one-word statements with each having its own uniqueness depending on context and usage. "Sober-minded" (*nephalion*) means temperate or more literally "unmixed with wine." "Self-controlled" (*sophrona*) means prudent, proper, one who controls his passion and desires. The ability to exercise self-discipline is a key component to this qualification. "Respectable" (*kosmion*) carries the idea of well-ordered, mature, and modest believer. These three qualifications point to a well-ordered, self-disciplined life. "Hospitable" (*philoxenon*) is defined in the Greek as being hospitable and loving strangers. It is not an issue of friendliness. Rather, the overseer was to open his home to the persecuted believers as they fled the tyranny of Rome, and to missionaries and itinerate preachers spreading the gospel or even to strangers in need.

"Able to teach" (*didaktikon*) is the only term in Paul's list describing a pastoral function. It is only one word in the original language meaning one who is skillful in teaching. An overseer must have the ability to pass on advice and doctrine to enquirers in a manner they understand. This quality was highly regarded in the Graeco-Roman culture. *Everything rises and falls on leadership* is a maxim the apostle Paul seems to be in step with by giving the basic requirements for church leadership. The strength of the church would be dependent, to a large degree, on the character of its leadership.

Four of the five pastoral traits in verse 3 are stated in the negative. "Not a drunkard" (*paranion*) meaning not addicted to wine nor a heavy drinker, and "not violent" (*plekten*) describing someone who is a bully, a brawler, or a fierce aggressor. These two characteristics are reasons enough for rejecting a potential shepherd of the church. They demonstrate a life of excess and loss of control to the point where they may cause harm to themselves or others. The final two negative statements in verse 3 are "not quarrelsome" (*amachon*) and "not a lover of money" (*aphilargron*). Unpacking "not quarrelsome" paints a picture of a peaceful man who is not contentious or given to battles. This requirement also emphasizes verbal abuse while "not violent" points to physical abuse.

"Not a lover of money" does not mean church leaders should hate money. Money is a necessity of life and ministry. Paul would state "Let the elders that rule well be counted worthy of double honor…" (1 Timothy 5:17, KJV), which many believe is respect and remuneration. Paul's focus is on the motivation of the pastor who would desire shepherding the church for purely financial reward. Also, this qualification highlights the reoccurring theme in the New Testament of *contentment* (Hebrews 13:5; 1 Timothy 6:6-10). Biblical contentment is a conviction that acknowledges Christ's power and provision are far more than sufficient for any circumstance.

The only positive adjective in the verse is placed in the middle of the verse following not violent. It is the word "gentle" (*epieike*), which gently expresses the idea of tolerance, kindness, and graciousness. The pastor is not to be brash, rash, or given to excesses in life, whether it be alcohol or anger. His temperament should be calm and content.

First Timothy 3:4 redirects our attention back to the home. While verse 2 emphasizes faithfulness, the focus of this verse is the pastor's leadership and caring ability for his family. "Manage" (*proistamenon*) means to lead, to guide, to direct. Paul gives the church in search of a pastor the permission to look at his family. He is not just to lead; he is to lead *well* (*kalos*). Leading "well" is not a mediocre word. It speaks to something being done with excellence and beauty. The main point, however, is the phrase "with all dignity" (*semnotetos*), which describes how the leading and caring is done. Dignity demands an effective exercise of authority bolstered by a character of integrity and sensitive compassion. When used in verse 5 with the verb "care," it clarifies the quality of leading the home by showing mercy rather than by delivering ultimatums. The pastor is not to lead his family with an iron fist, rather, he is to lead with loving guidelines. Lack of proper leadership in the home is clearly grounds for disqualification of a man for the office of pastor.

Verse 5 states this qualification in a smaller to larger contrast. If a man does not know how to lead and care well for his family, then how well would he lead the church? This is a rhetorical question implying he cannot. It is interesting the verb used for a father ruling or leading his children is the same word used in other places for elders ruling or leading the church (1 Timothy 5:17; 1 Thessalonians 5:12; Romans 12:8). Again, to lead the church, the pastor must lead his children and family well.

Verse 6 of 1 Timothy 3 clearly teaches that the pastor should not be a recent convert. The length of time is not given. The word "recent" (*neophyton*) paints a picture of a newly planted or young plant. Sufficient time is needed for a believer to learn, mature, and produce fruit for others to see before he is ready to fulfill the office of pastor. If time is not given the new convert may be "puffed up" with pride and fall into Satan's traps.

The final qualification is to be well thought of by others outside the church (verse 7). In our day, it may be hard to find someone "well thought of by outsiders" (*echo kalos martyria apo ho exothen)* because so many outside the church do not think well of the church or pastor in any regard. Yet, the challenge is to find someone with faithful and sound character who would appeal to those outside the church. Obviously, those outside the church do not choose church leadership, but the pastor is to have the character to favorably represent the church and gain the trust of those who have little confidence in the church. The end of the verse has a similar warning as the end of verse 6. The meaning of the phrase devil's trap or judgment remains ambiguous. Outlaw suggests "the 'snare of the devil' is "the reproach which the pastor will fall into without a good testimony among the community ... If a pastor's life does not measure up ... [the community] will not respect or listen to him publicly or privately."[2]

Looking back at the daunting list, it is amazing there are *any* pastors! Even though the list is given mostly in one-word statements without explanation in the text, it is still formidable. Yet, there is nothing in the text that seems to give any single qualification more weight than any of the others.

Husband of One Wife

Now, we will briefly examine the literary and cultural context of the phrase "husband of one wife" and possible (and some improbable) meanings.

There are four steps to basic biblical interpretation.[3] The first question to ask is, "What did the text mean to the original audience?" The answer starts with a good understanding of the literary style or genre of the book in which the text is found. Next, become familiar with the historical context of the era and study key words in the text.

The second question to consider is, "What are the differences between the biblical audience and us?" We are separated from the author's intended audience by time, culture, language, situation, and sometimes covenant. The key is to look for the significant differences between our situation today and the situation of the original biblical audience in their culture.

Third, we must discern, "What is the biblical principle in the text?" The interpreter's task is not to read the text within the context of our day, or to create our own meaning. The job is to discover the meaning intended by the author. The goal is to unearth the specifics of the text and then look for universal principles to guide us in the present. A good biblical principle will reflect the text, agree with the rest of Scripture, be timeless, and not be culturally bound.

Finally, we must grasp the text in our setting. The question is, "How should Christians apply the principle today?" A text may yield several biblical principles and there will be many possible applications. The application of the text may look different from believer to believer depending on our life situation and our maturity in Christ.

All four questions set the backdrop for a closer look at the "husband of one wife" qualification (1 Timothy 3:2). Again, the Greek reads *mias gynaikos andra*, which translates "one woman man." Paul wrote this phrase to Timothy without a verb or without any further explanation. We can safely assume that both men understood the intent of the phrase. However, their comprehension does not bring much clarity to the discussion for us. Had Paul inserted the word for divorce much of the ambiguity would have been removed. He did not. But we are not without direction. We begin by looking at the text in light of the culture of Paul's day.

Interpretations of "One Woman Man"

Bible scholars propose at least five possible ways to interpret *mias gynaikos andra*. One option is to interpret this text as a mandate for the pastor to be married. This question is addressed in chapter 2 (Manning). The question of polygamy, another common interpretation, is discussed in chapter 4 (Blair).

Another possibility contends Paul was addressing the issue of multiple sexual relationships, also known as concubinage. Even though there were laws discouraging this practice, sexual promiscuity was common. Archeologists have discovered some marriage contracts during this time with promises to avoid it. Polyamorous relationships are not an invention of our time; unfortunately, having multiple sexual partners has been part of many cultures throughout history. In Ephesus, however, history suggests concubinage was not a common practice, and therefore, this issue is an unlikely contender for Paul's original intent.

The fourth possibility is the issue of a second wife. Those who hold this position believe that a pastor should not have more than one wife in a lifetime. This limitation could include those who have experienced the death of a spouse or have experienced divorce. In the case of the death of a spouse, Paul instructs that remarriage is allowed (Roman 7:1-3; 1 Corinthians 7:39).

The last possibility is the issue of faithfulness. The "one woman man" is held to the high standard of being fully devoted to his wife. The key principle of faithfulness is consistent with the entire emphasis of 1 Timothy 3. Paul is requiring the pastor to be faithful to the one woman he is married to. The Jews and Romans both valued faithfulness to their spouse and family. If he was faithful to his wife then he would certainly, in the culture of Paul's day, be well thought of by those outside the church. The issue of faithfulness seems to fit the text well.

First Timothy 5:9-10 will prove interesting at this point. Paul is discussing the church's ministry of care for the widows in the congregation. Those who would receive church resources had to meet a set of requirements: being 60+ years old, being a "one husband woman" (with the same wording in a different order found in 1 Timothy 3:2), have a reputation for doing good, live above reproach, have a good reputation, hospitable to strangers, helping the distressed, and faithful to commit themselves to every good work. The list is very similar to the qualifications of the pastor. If, to be consistent in interpretation, the pastor cannot be divorced, then a widow who wishes to receive church financial support must not be divorced, either. The context of both 1 Timothy 3:2-7 and 1 Timothy 5:9-10 appear to highlight the issue of personal faithfulness to God more than offer a clear and concise teaching on divorce.

Conclusion

Relatively speaking, few passages speak to the issue of divorce. What is clear: God hates divorce (Malachi 2:16), yet God made exceptions for it in the Old Testament Law (Deuteronomy 21:10-14). Jesus hates divorce, yet He made an exception that allows a divorce because of adultery (Matthew 5:31-32). Paul hates divorce yet under the inspiration of the Holy Spirit made what has been dubbed the "Pauline Provision" that permits divorce due to the abandonment of a spouse (1 Corinthians 7:10-15). Scripture consistently stands against divorce, yet exceptions are made that allow it. Whether these exceptions apply to the pastor is yet another issue of interpretation.

The question remains, when a pastoral search committee or congregation looks for a pastor, why does the issue of divorce seem to be weighted more than the other qualifications? It seems that the number one criterion for disqualification almost exclusively deals with the issue of divorce. Divorce can be a disqualifier but so could being dishonest, consistently contentious, possessing a bullyish disposition, or having a lack of self-control. For whatever reason, the other biblical qualifications for ministry are often minimized or overlooked. Obviously, divorce is an easy fact to check; while issues such as being hospitable, apt to teach, or manages his house well are more difficult to discern in the brief interview process.

More than one qualification exists for pastoring a church. From the various qualification lists, one item does not appear any more important than the others in Paul's order, context, or language. Each is equally inspired by the Holy Spirit in the context of the original audience and certainly applicable for us today. Again, 1 Timothy 3:2-7 strongly suggests faithfulness is the key. If a search committee ignores the totality and theme of the qualifications in 1 Timothy 3, the church will suffer, and reproach will come to the cause of Christ.

The escapades and failures of prominent ministers make local and national news and will even go viral on social media. But the greater concern is the damage and pain they cause, which ultimately brings repudiation to the name of Christ. In recent years, high-profile pastors have deeply wounded their local church and the cause of Christ in their community. While these pastors met the standard of a "one woman man," their issues with aggressive anger, a quarrelsome spirit, and bullying, hurt people, wrecked the church, and destroyed lives. Those loyal to the pastor tried to excuse his sins, while those who opposed him tried to seize an opportunity for a forced exit, resulting in more conflict in the church and reproach to the cause of Christ. In other situations, good preachers who passed the litmus test of having only one wife lacked self-control or rose to a level of prominence where pride or "the love of money" consumed them to the point of moral compromise. Such failures cause others to struggle to this day. These issues can have eternal consequences.

Churches may give pastoral candidates the benefit of the doubt on some issues, thinking they have grown past them and learned from them. If all the qualifications in the 1 Timothy 3 list have equal standing, then why is the divorced candidate not given the same consideration as having learned and grown through his personal experiences?

Some people believe a divorced pastor will be at a disadvantage when counseling those with marital issues. They hold to the argument that because divorce was experienced in the past, there is no moral standing to counsel or teach people with marital issues in the present. If true, then pastors who struggled in past with losing their temper—and this is many of us—have no moral standing to counsel or teach on anger, self-control, or being quarrelsome. This same line of reasoning applies for all the qualifications in 1 Timothy and Titus. Could it be that pastors who have struggled with and worked through sinful or painful issues are just as able, if not more so, to spot the issue, address the struggle, and give hope? The basis of biblical teaching is the inspired Word of God not our personal experiences.

No one is suggesting the church lower its standards or compromise God's Word. What is being suggested is we reengage the Scriptures to give this issue a fresh look. There are a variety of biblical viewpoints to be discussed. Study the Scripture. Reach out to the struggling ministers you know, listen to their story. Process it with other pastors. Think. Give grace. Let all the Scripture be your guide.

Endnotes

[1] Qualifications of the description of the military general in *Strategikos* by Onasander are similar to terms used in 1 Timothy 3 (self-restrained, being a good father, and of good reputation) according to Knight, G. W. (1992). *The Pastoral Epistles: A Commentary on the Greek* (Grand Rapids, MI; Carlisle, England: W. B. Eerdmans; Paternoster Press), 151.

[2] W. Stanley Outlaw, "1 Timothy" in *1 Thessalonians Through Philemon*, ed. Robert E. Picirilli. The Randall House Bible Commentary (Nashville, TN: Randall House, 1990), 223-224).

[3] For a creative illustration of these principles, see Duvall, J. Scott & J. Daniel Hayes. *Grasping God's Word: A Hands-On Approach to Reading Interpreting, and Applying the Bible* (Grand Rapids, MI: Zondervan, 2005), 22-25.

CHAPTER FOUR

Is Polygamy Part of the Equation?

By Jeff Blair, D.Min.,
pastor, Locust Grove Free Will Baptist Church,
Locust Grove, Oklahoma

> *Do you have more than one living wife? (This question appears in many of our association's ministerial question-naires.) Through the years the phrase has been used so often some may even believe that it is a biblical phrase, word for word from the Scriptures.*—Doug Carey

Such is clearly not the case, and this book is evidence that there are unsettled questions around this issue. For instance, Did the apostle Paul intend to prohibit polygamy[1] for pastors when he penned the phrase in 1 Timothy 3:2, *mias gynaikos andra,* variously translated as "husband of one wife" (KJV, et al), "married only once" (NRSV), "faithful to his wife" (NIV, et al), among others. If Paul was forbidding polygamy for pastors, then is a man who has been divorced and remarried guilty of polygamy and, therefore, disqualified from the role of pastor? If, however, Paul was not addressing the matter of polygamy, what did he mean by this phrase? These are the questions considered in this chapter.

As the reader likely knows well already, this topic is fraught with *exegetical* ambiguities and *pastoral* quandaries, and both aspects of the

issue are critically important, for we are not dealing merely with passages of Scripture but also with people in specific situations. Sometimes
a man's reputation, calling, and ministry hang in the balance. Therefore,
this discussion is not to be entered into unadvisedly or lightly, understanding that we are dealing with the complexities of real life and not in
abstractions. Decisions must be made, and we may not have all of the
answers we might hope to possess.

Texts are neither penned nor applied in cultural-historical vacuums,
so the wisdom and sensitivity of pastor-theologians with feet firmly
planted in the worlds of both the first and the twenty-first centuries are
required.

With these things in mind, I chart the course for this chapter. Section
one, "Polygamy's History," examines polygamy in its Old Testament
canonical context to get a sense of the trajectory of this practice in early
Israelite history. Section two, "Polygamy in Paul's Context," considers
the texts from the Second Temple period to understand how the thinking
about and practice of polygamy had developed through the first century
CE. Section three, "Polygamy in Paul's Text," zeros in on the phrase
in 1 Timothy 3:2 and evaluate it in light of the cultural environment of
first century Ephesus, the context of the Pauline corpus, specifically the
book of 1 Timothy. In the last section, "Interpretation and Application
of the Text in Context," I offer my exegetical conclusions and practical
application.

Polygamy's History

Genesis 2:18-23 narrates the union of the first man and first woman.
Uncharacteristic of Hebrew narrative, in verse 24 the author then spells
out for the hearer/reader the enduring meaning of what has been described, "Therefore a man shall leave his father and his mother and hold
fast to his wife, and *they* shall become one flesh" (Genesis 2:24, emphasis mine). The commentary signifies that this wedding story points
beyond itself: marriage between man and woman is to be an abiding

pattern for humanity. Genesis 3 relates the account that is commonly referred to as the Fall. Sin with a capital "S" has been unleashed in the world through the rebellion of the first humans. Genesis then begins to detail the subsequent slide of humanity deeper and deeper into sin. In Genesis 4:18-24, we hear of the violent and arrogant Lamech who is introduced to us in this way, "And Lamech took *two* wives" (verse 19a, emphasis mine). There is no encounter here between Lamech and Yahweh about this as in the previous episode in which God confronts Cain, first in warning, then in wrath (4:6-12). Beeson Divinity School professor of Old Testament, Kenneth A. Mathews, however, notes that Lamech's polygamy was a deviaton from God's creational design[2] and is a signpost on the slide further into the sin that eventually resulted in God's judgment in the Flood. Many discern in the Lamech narrative the beginning of a subtle yet consistent polemic against polygamy in the Hebrew Bible. Though Old Testament polygamists include no less than Abraham, Jacob, Gideon, Elkanah, Saul, David, Solomon, and Rehoboam *there are almost no reports of polygamy without problems plaguing the arrangement.* Jealousy and competition are the typical troubles generated by polygamy,[3] but in an extreme case, it was the named cause of the not-unforeseen pitfall of apostasy. Deuteronomy 17:17 warns the future Israelite kings against multiplying wives "lest his heart turn away,"[4] though in context the king is being warned against amassing weapons and wealth in addition to women,[5] and is unlikely to have understood this command as limiting the king to one wife only (although see below "Qumran's interpretation"). While it is true, as Kaiser pointed out that permission for polygamy is never stated[6] it is also true that "polygamy was never made illegal."[7] There is no law in the Old Testament explicitly prohibiting polygamy. In a number of places, in fact, *accommodation* is made for the practice. For instance, Exodus 21:9-11 requires a man who takes a second wife not to neglect the needs of his first wife.[8] Even more concerning is the speech of Yahweh through Nathan to David when he had committed adultery and murder. Yahweh said to David,

I anointed you king over Israel, and I delivered you out of
the hand of Saul. And I gave you your master's house and
your master's wives into your arms and gave you the house
of Israel and of Judah. And if this were too little, I would add
to you as much more... I will take your wives before your
eyes and give them to your neighbor, and he shall lie with
your wives in the sight of this sun (2 Samuel 12:7b-8, 11b;
emphasis mine).

In the context of David being confronted for *taking Uriah's wife*, it
seems to indicate that Yahweh had been responsible for giving Saul's
wives to David *as wives* and would have given David other wives in
addition to these if David had so desired.[9]

The data of the Old Testament led to the conclusion that though
monogamy is the creational ideal, and the practice of polygamy was
the cause of all manner of chaos and strife, Israel failed to sufficiently
embrace Yahweh's beautiful pattern for human marriage and insist on
monogamy in Israelite society. The evidence suggests that Israel was at
best marginally different than its pagan neighbors in their views on and
practice of polygamy.[10] During this period, the Law of Yahweh, though
never requiring or praising polygamy, nevertheless tolerated and made
accommodations for it in various ways.

Polygamy in Paul's Context

By the first century AD, there were several voices in the Jewish community speaking critically against polygamy. Documents found among
the Dead Sea Scrolls reflect a move toward strict monogamy. The Damascus Document[11] 4.20–5.6 says,

The 'builders of the wall'[12] (Ezek. 13:10)...shall be caught
in fornication twice by taking a second wife while the first is
alive, whereas the principle of creation is, *Male and female*

created He them (Genesis 1:27). And concerning the prince
it is written, *He shall not multiply wives to himself* (Deuteronomy 17:17)

This sectarian exegete goes back to the beginning (Genesis 1:27), to
"the principle of creation" to begin to build his case against polygamy,
which reinforces that monogamy is Yahweh's design for everybody.

Paul's thinking on this also would have been profoundly influenced
by the teaching of Jesus. In Mark 10:2-12 and Matthew 19:3-12, Jesus
teaches that monogamy is Yahweh's creational, normative will. Notice
the strategy and emphasis of Jesus in Mark 10:2-9:

> And Pharisees came up and in order to test him asked, "Is it
> lawful for a man to divorce his wife?" He answered them,
> "What did Moses command you?" They said, "Moses al-
> lowed a man to write a certificate of divorce and to send her
> away." And Jesus said to them, "Because of your hardness of
> heart he wrote you this commandment. But from *the begin-
> ning of creation, 'God made them male and female.'* 'There-
> fore a man shall leave his father and mother and hold fast to
> his wife, and the two shall become one flesh.' So they are
> no longer two but one flesh. What therefore God has joined
> together, let not man separate" (emphasis mine).

This text and its parallel in Matthew are foundational for the Christian view of sexuality. They address not only the question of divorce,
which is the subject of the text, but also have implications for the Christian ethical views of homosexuality and polygamy. For our discussion,
we note that Jesus went back to the beginning, Genesis 1:27, just as
the Damascus Document did. Before the Fall, "from the beginning of
creation" the standard was established: one man united by God with
one woman in the one-flesh union. Jesus emphasized the "two-ness"
by twice quoting (verse 8) the reference to Genesis 2:24. It seems clear
from 1 Corinthians 7:10-11 that Paul knew this teaching of Jesus.

Even with growing voices of dissent, mainstream Judaism in the land of Israel continued to hold that polygamy was permissible, though monogamy was no doubt the typical arrangement for most families. In the second half of the first century AD, Josephus maintained that "it is the ancient practice among us to have many wives at the same time."[13] In the second century, the Christian apologist, Justin Martyr, in chapter 133 of his *Dialogue of Justin with Trypho, a Jew,* criticized the Jews for continuing to practice polygamy, saying,

> If, then, the teaching of the prophets and of Himself moves you, it is better for you to follow God than your imprudent and blind masters, who even till this time permit each man to have four or five wives; and if any one see a beautiful woman and desire to have her, they quote the doings of Jacob [called] Israel, and of the other patriarchs, and maintain that it is not wrong to do such things.[14]

In Paul's day, there was a stream of tradition beginning to form within Judaism to return to Yahweh's creational design for marriage. The apostle Paul no doubt would have known this tradition due to his acquaintance with the Septuagint (and possibly other versions), which he had likely committed to memory,[15] but more importantly and decisively, Paul knew this tradition from King Jesus. Paul was trained as a Pharisee in Jerusalem at the feet of the eminent Gamaliel (Acts 22:3), but he had been converted to Christ Jesus and sent by the Lord into the Greco-Roman world as the "apostle to the Gentiles" (Romans 11:13; Ephesians 3:1-10). It is to this world we now turn.

Polygamy in Paul's Text?

Paul wrote 1 Timothy to Timothy to whom Paul had given the charge to deal with a number of issues in the church in the city of Ephesus (1:3), a large and important city in western Asia Minor, modern day

Turkey. In 1 Timothy 3, Paul gave instructions regarding the expectations for a person being considered as *episkopos*, which means overseer or pastor. It is here that we find the phrase under investigation, "Therefore an overseer must be above reproach, *(mias gynaikos andra)* the husband of one wife…" Did Paul, in this phrase, intend to prohibit the practice of polygamy for pastors?

This understanding is attractive for a couple of reasons. First, *clarity* of the wording. A. T. Robertson, renowned Greek scholar and long-time professor at Southern Seminary, in his widely-used *Word Pictures*, laconically comments, "*mias gunaikos*. One at a time, clearly."[16] Likewise, New Testament Greek expert, Bill Mounce, though he finally doubts this interpretation, admits that polygamy "is the most natural understanding of *mias gunaikos*, 'one woman.'"[17] Perhaps it is even natural for the reader to supply the words, "one woman *at a time*."

Second, this interpretation was held by some in *antiquity*. The renowned scholar and preacher of the fourth century, John Chrysostom states, "This he does not lay down as a rule, as if he must not be without one, but as *prohibiting his having more than one*. For even the Jews were allowed to contract second marriages, and even to have two wives at one time."[18] We also know that Paul utilized the rendering of Genesis 2:24 that emphasizes that "two" become one in 1 Corinthians 6:16 and Ephesians 5:32, where he quotes Genesis 2:24 as "the *two* shall be one flesh." These things might lead one to the conclusion that polygamy is, in fact, the central target in this text.

Most New Testament scholars, however, do not believe the polygamy interpretation is plausible.[19] Why is this the case? This hesitancy rests on at least two considerations. *First*, Paul uses the opposite phrase in 1 Timothy 5:9, *henos andros gynē,* "one-man woman," to describe the requirements of widows to be placed on the widow's list to receive support from church. If polygamy is the point of 1 Timothy 3:2, due to the similarity of phrasing, consistency would require us to invest both phrases with the same sense. Polyandry—a wife having several husbands at one time—however, was not practiced in that culture, and was certainly not in view here.[20] Therefore it is highly unlikely that polygamy was Paul's primary meaning in 3:2. *Second*, the Greco-Roman culture in which Ephesus was situated "held to a strict monogamy."[21] In fact, Keener noted that polygamy was a violation of Roman law and one who was guilty would at least be viewed as *infamia*, and certainly would not qualify as "above reproach."[22] The overarching qualification for the pastor in 1 Timothy 3:1-7 is that he be "above reproach." Therefore, to have these two qualifications listed side by side would have been something of a tautology. Outside of the region of Judea, Jewish people avoided polygamy, in accordance with the typical Greek practice. Since in Asia neither the Jews nor the Greeks practiced polygamy, there would have been little reason for Paul to address that issue in his letter to church leaders there. Therefore, "husband of one wife" is not merely a prohibition of polygamy.[23]

For the Ephesians, monogamy would have been in the category of what the German sociologist Arnold Gehlen called a "background institution." A background institution is one which is taken for granted and requires no deliberation. For instance, in our culture, wearing clothes in public is a background institution. In the morning, we walk into the closet and must decide *which* clothes to wear; none of us—hopefully!—ponder anew each day whether or not we will wear *any* clothes. If you were to ask an Ephesian husband, "Is this your only wife?" He would have responded, "Of course." "Of course" answers are in the realm of background institutions. Monogamy was one of those institutions, and therefore required no prohibition.[24]

The important point here is that a prohibition of polygamy is implied or taken for granted but would not have been the primary target of Paul's instruction. Paul's background as a follower of Jesus would have agreed with the Greco-Roman practice of disallowing polygamy—though obviously for different reasons—but it is not Paul's primary purpose here. So, polygamy is "part of the equation," to use the lingo of the chapter title, but we must look elsewhere for the point. The phrase in context cannot be less than a prohibition of polygamy; it must be more. What is the *more*?

The Interpretation and Application
of the Text in Context

It seems to me that the most plausible meaning of *mias gynaikos andra* is "a man who is faithful to his wife." Paul meant this in a *qualitative* rather than a *quantitative* sense. The pastor must, of course, have no more than one wife at the same time, but the entire qualification depends on *the kind of husband he is to his one and only wife*. As Lenski argues, "The emphasis is on *one* wife's husband, and the sense is that he has nothing to do with any other woman. He must be a man who cannot be taken hold of[25] on the score of sexual promiscuity or laxity… a man who is not strictly faithful to his one wife is debarred."[26] Lenski rightly points to the first century Ephesian context in which monogamy was taken for granted, as were frequenting prostitutes, having sex with one's slaves, concubines, mistresses, and "all the rest of the vileness that formed the soil from which these grew."[27] All manner of sexual promiscuity was common in the Greco-Roman world, and no doubt many of the converts to Christianity had been mired in such a lifestyle (1 Corinthians 6:9-20). The Christian pastor, then, was required to be much more than merely monogamous; he was expected to be holy and faithful.

If this is the correct understanding of the phrase, the question naturally arises, "Who, then, may be considered a 'one-woman man?'" Though in my view Wayne Grudem reaches an incorrect conclusion,[28] his approach to this text is the right one. He notes that all the other qualifications in this list describe "a man's *present status*," not "one who has *never* been," but one who is "not now."[29]

The upshot for Grudem is that 1 Timothy 3:2 does not, then, necessarily disqualify from the pastorate men who have been divorced and subsequently married to another woman. Craig Keener reaches the same conclusion, "'Husband of one wife' refers to one's current marital status and behavior; validly divorced people who remarried were considered married to one spouse, the second one, not to two spouses."[30] It is possible for a man who has been divorced and remarried to be considered a "one-woman man." The constraints of this chapter do not allow an in-depth exploration of the biblical data on divorce and remarriage. Here I will merely summarize what I take to be the biblical teaching on the subject as it relates to our question.

The overwhelming thrust of the Bible vis-à-vis marriage and divorce is that divorce is always a sin and a tragedy. The reason divorce is a sin is that Yahweh is a God of *chesed* (חֶסֶד) loyal love, who does not break covenant with His beloved. Divorce is alien to the nature of God. Yahweh established marriage to be a permanent, one-flesh union between one man and one woman for life. Deuteronomy 24:1-4, however, articulates the requirements laid upon a man who divorces his wife. Subsequent Jewish interpreters disagreed about the meaning of this passage. This discussion between the two primary authorities in the first century, Hillel and Shammai, is found in Mishnah Gittin 9.10:

A   The House of Shammai say, "A man should divorce his wife only because he has found grounds for it in unchastity,

B   "since it is said, *Because he has found in her indecency in anything* (Dt. 24:1)."

C   And the House of Hillel say, "Even if she spoiled his dish,

D   "since it is said, *Because he has found in her indecency in anything.*

E   R. Aqiba says, "Even if he found someone else prettier than she,

F   "since it is said, *And it shall be if she find no favor in his eyes* (Dt. 24:1)."[31]

Shammai understood Deuteronomy 24:1 to mean that the only legal ground for divorce was if the wife was unfaithful to the husband. The house of Hillel taught that the phrase, "she finds no favor in his eyes because he has found some indecency in her" to mean that if the wife does anything displeasing to her husband, he has the legal right to send her away with a bill of divorce; the husband could divorce his wife for any and every reason, or "for any cause." The following passage in Josephus reflects this background,

> He that desires to be divorced from his wife for any cause whatsoever (and many such causes happen among men), let him in writing give assurance that he will never use her as his wife any more; for by this means she may be at liberty to marry another husband, although before this bill of divorce be given, she is not to be permitted so to do.[32]

The disagreement between Hillel and Shammai in the first century is the background to the pericope in Matthew 19:3-9 (the parallel of Mark 10, above),

> And Pharisees came up to him and tested him by asking, "Is it lawful to divorce one's wife *for any cause*?" He answered, "Have you not read that he who created them from the beginning made them male and female, and said, 'Therefore a man shall leave his father and his mother and hold fast to his wife, and the two shall become one flesh'? So they are no longer two but one flesh. What therefore God has joined together, *let not man separate*." They said to him, "Why then did Moses command one to give a certificate of divorce and to send her away?" He said to them, "Because of your hardness of heart Moses allowed you to divorce your wives, but *from the beginning it was not so*. And I say to you: whoever divorces his wife, except for sexual immorality, and marries another, commits adultery" (emphasis mine).

The meaning of the question in verse 3 is not, "Are there *any grounds* on which a man may divorce his wife?" but, "Is it legal for a man to divorce his wife *for any and every reason* he may deem appropriate?" In His response, Jesus went back to the beginning to emphasize Yahweh's creational, pre-Fall pattern for marriage. As we have seen, Yahweh intended marriage to be between one man and one woman for life. Divorce was an accommodation for the fallen nature of humanity, "Because of your hardness of heart" (verse 8). The point of contention among Christian interpreters is the significance of the exception clause in verse 9, "except for sexual immorality." Did Jesus here allow remarriage for a person who divorced on the ground of sexual unfaithfulness of his/her spouse? I quote the New Testament scholar, Bill Heth, here because his is an interesting case. Dr. Heth for many years was considered one of the foremost defenders of the so-called "no divorce and remarriage" view. After further reflection, he changed his mind[33] and begin to defend the view that legitimate divorces included the right to remarry.[34]

It seems compelling to me that in Matthew 19 the exception clause of Jesus would have been understood in that cultural context to allow the victim of divorce to remarry without being guilty of sin. Furthermore, in 1 Corinthians 7:15 Paul, dealing with a different set of concrete circumstances, says to the Christian whose spouse abandons her, "But if the unbelieving partner separates, let it be so. In such cases the brother or sister is *not enslaved.* God has called you to peace" (emphasis mine). Paul evidently knew the saying of Jesus we know from Mark 10, which he alludes to in 1 Corinthians 7:10, yet in 7:15 Paul, in a different context, allows for another exception, in addition to the one in Matthew 19, to the "no divorce" principle,[35] and says that in the event that the Christian is abandoned, he or she is "not enslaved," which I take to mean, "free to remarry."[36] I think it is important to notice with respect to the one-flesh marriage relationship, that although Jesus stresses the fact that it is God who has joined the two together, Jesus does not infer from this fact that man *cannot* separate it. The clause in Matthew 19:6b is in the imperative, not in the indicative, "Let not man separate." For a human being to separate what God has joined together is both a transgression and a tragedy, but not an impossibility. If it is possible for the one-flesh relationship to be broken, then remarriage does not constitute polygamy.[37]

Clearly there is much more to be said concerning the details of divorce and remarriage. Here I have attempted to briefly sketch my reading. With this summary in view, I want to return to the question I raised above, "*Who, then, may be considered a one-woman man?*" First, obviously, a man who has been married only one time *may* meet this qualification, though I want to emphasize that since being a "one-woman man" depends on the *kind* of husband a man is to his wife, having only one wife is insufficient to establish that a man is, in fact, a "one-woman man." Paul is raising the bar, not lowering it. More on this in just a moment. Second, a man who has never been married but who meets the rest of the qualifications. (This question is considered in depth in chapter two.) Third, a man who was married but has been widowed (see Romans 7:1-3). Fourth, a man who was the victim of a broken marriage and is now either single or is a faithful husband to his present wife. I must stress here—and I want the reader to lean forward and pay close attention—in keeping with the emphasis and thrust of the biblical material, a man (or woman) who finds himself in a situation in which divorce is allowed must never think that divorce is required, and the teaching of Jesus on forgiveness—7 x 70—applies here. Jesus calls us to do everything within our power to keep the marriage together, for "what God has joined together, let not man separate." Fifth... is there a fifth? I do believe there is a fifth. I am convinced that the sweep of Holy Scripture allows us, invites us, to imagine the possibility of ministry even for a man who is guilty. The truth is, we all are, for who among us has been all these things (1 Timothy 3:1-7) all of the time? This fact does not diminish the practical necessity of holding leaders to a higher degree of accountability. This is biblical and undeniable (James 3:1), and sometimes that means discipline is necessary; but it *should* cause each of us to place ourselves again in the shoes of the tax collector with his head low and never the Pharisee looking down upon him. I believe this is right because I believe the walk of Jesus with Peter on the shore that morning has broad application, for I turn the page, and Peter is restored and preaching to the Pentecostal crowds by the power of the Spirit.

This does not mean that the process of restoration for a man who has been unfaithful is an easy one. It is not. Depending on the nature of the transgression, it may require years of rehabilitation of his character and reputation before full restoration becomes a reality. Spurgeon's words early in his book, *Lectures to My Students*, are apropos and, in my opinion, establish a wise course,

> As John Angell James remarks "When a preacher of righteousness has stood in the way of sinners, he should never again open his lips in the great congregation *until his repentance is as notorious as his sin*." Let those who have been shorn by the sons of Ammon tarry at Jericho til their beards be grown... Alas! The beard of reputation once shorn is hard to grow again... my belief is that we should be very slow to help back to the pulpit men, who having been once tried, have proved themselves to have too little grace to stand the crucial test of ministerial life.[38]

Many will wonder how this is to be done. What are the rules? Finally, it must be discerned within particular communities. This is not neat. Living in communities governed by grace over law always requires more wisdom. It is no doubt easier to live in a community based on law rather than on grace, but such a place would not be the Church of God. There is no formula into which one might plug the variables and get an answer. It is based on Scripture and involves relationship, knowing in community, patience, and wisdom. We must also come to terms with the lamentable fact that in some cases the sin will be such that restoration to the previous position of pastor will be impossible,[39] though forgiveness is, of course, not out of reach for anyone who would repent. Some of these issues are addressed in chapter five.

The following points summarize the answer to the initial question for this chapter:

1. Polygamy was not God's creational pattern. It is a post-Fall reality and in the Old Testament is typically portrayed in a negative light. It is, however, nowhere in the Old Testament unambiguously forbidden.

2. Polygamy was still practiced in Judean Jewish culture in the first century AD, though there was a tendency in some quarters in the period to criticize polygamy and emphasize the ethic of Genesis 2 (the Creation narrative).

3. Jesus closed the possibility of polygamy for God's people by appealing to the Genesis creational pattern and emphasizing the "*two*" becoming "one" aspect of the one-flesh language.

4. Paul's Greco-Roman context in Ephesus would not have required a prohibition of polygamy *because it was not practiced in that culture*. Monogamy would have been taken for granted. Polygamy, therefore, would have been only implicitly disallowed, though in light of the teaching of Jesus and the creational pattern, Paul would have upheld monogamy as normative. Since the *mias gynaikos andra* phrase *assumes* rather than *requires* that polygamy not be practiced, the primary application of the phrase must be found elsewhere.

5. The language and context of 1 Timothy 3 seem to indicate that the phrase *mias gynaikos andra* should be understood in a *qualitative* rather than a *quantitative* sense, addressing the *kind* of husband rather than the *number* wives. Qualification for the pastoral office vis-à-vis marriage depends, then, on the quality of the candidate's character, not the quantity of the candidate's marriage companions.

6. Though both Jesus and Paul insist on the sanctity of marriage and view all divorce as a sinful calamity, they also allow for some exceptions to the prohibition of divorce and remarriage. For them, it is possible, though tragic, for the one-flesh union to be dissolved. Since there are cases in which divorce and remarriage are allowed, and since *mias gynaikos andra* describes the "kind of" man the pastor should be, it is *possible* for a man who has been divorced and remarried to be qualified to be pastor in the church of God.

Perhaps it would be meaningful in conclusion to consider that 1 Timothy was written to Timothy and the church *at Ephesus*. There are some questions regarding the date and original recipients of the book of Ephesians,[40] but it is probably the case that the church at Ephesus had already in their possession these words which pastors often read in the wedding ceremonies we officiate, and I can imagine these words ringing in the ears of the Ephesians as they hear Paul's call for "one-woman kind of men,"

> *Husbands, love your wives, as Christ loved the church and gave himself up for her,* that he might sanctify her, having cleansed her by the washing of water with the word, so that he might present the church to himself in splendor, without spot or wrinkle or any such thing, that she might be holy and without blemish. In the same way husbands should love their wives as their own bodies. He who loves his wife loves himself. For no one ever hated his own flesh, but nourishes and cherishes it, just as Christ does the church, because we are members of his body. *"Therefore a man shall leave his father and mother and hold fast to his wife, and the two shall become one flesh."* This mystery is profound, and I am saying that it refers to Christ and the church. However, let each one of you love his wife as himself, and let the wife see that she respects her husband (Ephesians 5:25-33, emphasis mine).

Endnotes

1. For clarification, *polygamy* is multiple marriages at one time; *polygyny* is having multiple wives at one time; *polyandry* is multiple husbands at the same time.
2. Kenneth. A. Mathews, *Genesis 1–11:26*, 1A, *NAC* (Nashville, TN: Broadman & Holman, 1996), 285. So also Bruce K. Waltke, *Genesis: A Commentary* (Grand Rapids, MI: Zondervan, 2001), 100, "The escalation of sin is now extended to the marital relationship. Polygamy is a rejection of God's marital plan." Victor P. Hamilton, *The Book of Genesis, Chapters 1–17*, *The New International Commentary on the Old Testament* (*NICOT*) (Grand Rapids, MI: Eerdmans, 1990), 238.
3. E.g., between Sarah and Hagar (Genesis 16:3ff.), Jacob's wives (Genesis 29:31-30:24), Hannah and Peninnah (1 Samuel 1:3ff).
4. In Deuteronomy 7:4, the rationale for the command against the sons of Israel taking foreign wives is that "they would turn away your sons from following me, to serve other gods." First Kings 11:1ff. quotes Deuteronomy 7 in its condemnation of Solomon's sin of marrying many foreign women who turned his heart away from Yahweh.
5. Christopher J. H. Wright, *Deuteronomy*, *Understanding the Bible Commentary Series* (*UBCS*) (Grand Rapids, MI: Baker Books, 2012), 209.
6. Walter Kaiser, Jr. *Toward an Ethics of the Old Testament* (Grand Rapids, MI: Zondervan, 1991), 183. It seems to me that Kaiser's argument that "polygamy is expressly prohibited by God in his ordination of the institution of marriage in Genesis 2:24" (186) and that God sent the flood upon the earth because of man's "autocratic and polygamous ways" (183) goes beyond the evidence of the text.
7. Some have contended that Leviticus 18:18 is a prohibition of polygamy, but the lexical and contextual evidence for this position is weak. The prohibition seems straight forward: a man may not marry a woman's sister while she is living, for the sister will be considered a rival. See Jacob Milgrom, *Leviticus 17–22: A New Translation With Introduction and Commentary*, 3A, *The Anchor Yale Bible Commentaries* (*AYB*) (New Haven, CT: Yale University Press, 2008), 1549 for this understanding and the alternative interpretations.
8. "Thus the covenant law tolerated second wives, whether servants or not, but only if they were treated equally." Douglas K. Stuart, *Exodus*, vol. 2, *The New American Commentary* (*NAC*) (Nashville, TN: Broadman & Holman, 2006), 483. See also John I. Durham, *Exodus*, vol. 3, *Word Biblical Commentary* (*WBC*) (Dallas, TX: Word, 1987), 322.
9. "In light of the monogamous ideal outlined in Genesis 2:22-24, the gift of 'wives' in vv. 8, 11 would seem to be a divine concession to the polygamy that was relatively common (at least among the upper classes) in ancient Near Eastern culture." Ronald F. Youngblood, "1, 2 Samuel," *Expositor's Bible Commentary* (*EBC*), 3 (Grand Rapids, MI: Zondervan, 1992), 944. This was the understanding of Josephus as well, "God… who… had given him such wives as he had justly and legally married." Flavius Josephus and William Whiston, *The Works of Josephus: Complete and Unabridged* (Peabody, MA: Hendrickson, 1987), 192. Antiquities 7.151.

[10] "There is therefore no discernible distinctiveness between the Pentateuch and the ancient Near Eastern sources with regard to monogamy/polygamy." Instone-Brewer, *Divorce*, Loc. 267. "Marriage and its associated customs in the Old Testament were similar to those in Old Babylonia." Gordon J. Wenham, *Jesus, Divorce, and Remarriage: In Their Historical Setting* (Bellingham, WA: Lexham, 2020), 24.

[11] Also known as the Zadokite Fragment and abbreviated CD, the document is likely from the second century BC, c. 100 years before the birth of Jesus.

[12] Solomon Schechter suggested that the "Builders of the wall" against whom this passage is directed were the Pharisees whose motto, codified in Avot 1:1 was "Make a fence for the Torah." Solomon Schechter. *Documents of Jewish Sectaries*, 2 vols (Cambridge, England: Cambridge University Press, 1910), 1:xvii, as cited in Adela Yarbro Collins and Harold W. Attridge, *Mark: A Commentary, Hermeneia: a Critical and Historical Commentary on the Bible* (*Herm.*) (Minneapolis, MN: Fortress, 2007), 460. See also The Temple Scroll (11Q19) 57:17-18 for another Dead Sea Scrolls text condemning polygamy.

[13] Josephus, *Works*, 452. Antiquities 17.14

[14] Justin Martyr, "Dialogue of Justin with Trypho, a Jew," in *The Apostolic Fathers With Justin Martyr and Irenaeus*, ed. Alexander Roberts, James Donaldson, and A. Cleveland Coxe, 1, The Ante-Nicene Fathers (Buffalo, NY: Christian Literature Company, 1885), 266-267.

[15] So Ed Sanders concludes in his section on Paul's education, "Paul had probably memorized the Greek translation of Jewish Scripture." E. P. Sanders, *Paul: The Apostle' Life, Letters, and Thought* (Minneapolis, MN: Fortress, 2015), 73.

[16] A. T. Robertson, *Word Pictures in the New Testament* (Nashville, TN: Broadman, 1933), 1 Timothy 3:2.

[17] William D. Mounce, *Pastoral Epistles*, 46, *WBC* (Dallas, TX: Word, 2000), 171.

[18] John Chrysostom, "Homilies of St. John Chrysostom, Archbishop of Constantinople, on the First Epistle of St. Paul the Apostle to Timothy," in *Saint Chrysostom: Homilies on Galatians, Ephesians, Philippians, Colossians, Thessalonians, Timothy, Titus, and Philemon*, ed. Philip Schaff, trans. James Tweed and Philip Schaff, 13, A Select Library of the Nicene and Post-Nicene Fathers of the Christian Church, First Series (New York, NY: Christian Literature Company, 1889), 438. Emphasis mine. Chrysostom is followed by Calvin who comments, "The only true exposition, therefore, is that of Chrysostom, that in a bishop he expressly condemns polygamy." John Calvin and William Pringle, *Commentaries on the Epistles to Timothy, Titus, and Philemon* (Bellingham, WA: Logos Bible Software, 2010), 77.

[19] For a recent scholar who holds to the polygamy interpretation, see Wayne Grudem, *Systematic Theology: An Introduction to Biblical Doctrine* (Grand Rapids, MI: Zondervan, 1994), 917, who concludes, "It is best to understand 'the husband of one wife' to prohibit a polygamist from holding the office of elder [Grudem's translation of *episkopos*]. The verses say nothing about divorce and remarriage with respect to qualifications for church office."

[20] W. Stanley Outlaw, "1 Timothy" in *1 Thessalonians Through Philemon*, ed. Robert E. Picirilli. The Randall House Bible Commentary (Nashville, TN: Randall House, 1990), 217.

21 Instone-Brewer, *Divorce*, loc. 892-893.

22 Craig S. Keener, *...And Marries Another: Divorce and Remarriage in the Teaching of the New Testament* (Grand Rapids, MI: Baker Academic, 2012), 87-88. Emphasis in Keener, who cites here Jane F. Gardner, *Women in Roman Law & Society* (Bloomington, IN: Indiana University Press, 1986), 93. On the tradition of "Infamia" in Roman culture, see George Long, "INFA′MIA," ed. William Smith, *Dictionary of Greek and Roman Antiquities* (Boston, MA: Little, Brown, and Company, 1865), 635-636, who notes that "Infamia was a consequence of a man being at the same time in the relation of a double marriage."

23 Keener, *And Marries Another*, 88.

24 See Peter L. Berger and Anton C. Zijderveld, *In Praise of Doubt: How to Have Convictions Without Becoming a Fanatic* (New York, NY: HarperCollins, 2009), 13-16 for this idea and example.

25 His reference is to the first and overarching characteristic in the list, often translated "above reproach," literally "unable to be grasped/taken hold of."

26 R. C. H. Lenski, *The Interpretation of St. Paul's Epistles to the Colossians, to the Thessalonians, to Timothy, to Titus, and to Philemon* (Columbus, OH: Lutheran Book Concern, 1937), 581. Emphasis in the original. See also Thomas D. Lea and Hayne P. Griffin, *1, 2 Timothy, Titus*, 34, *NAC* (Nashville, TN: Broadman & Holman, 1992), 109-110, "It is better to see Paul having demanded that the church leader be faithful to his one wife. The Greek describes the overseer literally as a 'one-woman kind of man' (cf. "faithful to his one wife," NEB)." Philip H. Towner, *The Letters to Timothy and Titus*, New International Commentary on the New Testament (*NICNT*) (Grand Rapids, MI: Eerdmans, 2006), 251, "In such a context, the candidate's conduct within the marriage relationship (i.e. faithfulness to his wife) would be an anticipated topic." Luke Timothy Johnson, *The First and Second Letters to Timothy: A New Translation With Introduction and Commentary*, 35A, *The Anchor Yale Bible Commentaries* (*AYB*) (New Haven, CT; London, England: Yale University Press, 2008), 214, "Preceded as it is by the adjective 'blameless,' the main point of the requirement would seem to be first the avoidance of any appearance of immorality." William D. Mounce, *Pastoral Epistles*, 46, *WBC* (Dallas, TX: Word, 2000), 173, "The translation 'one-woman man' maintains the emphasis on "one" and carries over what seems to be Paul's emphasis on faithfulness." Ralph Earle, "1 Timothy," in *EBC*, ed. Frank E. Gaebelein, 11 (Grand Rapids, MI: Zondervan, 1981), 364, "Most commentators agree that it means monogamy—only one wife at one time—and that the overseer must be completely faithful to his wife." Gordon D. Fee, *1 and 2 Timothy, Titus*, *UBCS* (Grand Rapids, MI: Baker Books, 2011), 80, "It requires marital fidelity to his 'one wife.' In this view the 'overseer' is required to live an exemplary married life (marriage is assumed), faithful to his 'one wife' in a culture in which marital infidelity was common, and at times assumed." Raymond F. Collins, *1 & 2 Timothy and Titus: A Commentary*, *The New Testament Library* (*NTL*) (Louisville, KY: Westminster John Knox, 2012), 82, "He is urging that the would-be overseer be faithful to his wife." I. Howard Marshall, *The Pastoral Epistles*, International Critical Commentary (*ICC*) (London, England; New York, NY: T&T Clark, 1999) 478, *mias gynaikos andra* "is positive in tone and stresses faithfulness in marriage, rath-

er than prohibiting some specific unsanctioned form of marriage." Scot McKnight and Justine Gill, forthcoming *1 Corinthians*, New Cambridge Bible Commentary, "A 'one-woman-man' (or *married only once*; see, too, Tit 1:6) is underdetermined and could refer to being non-polygamous or not remarried (after a divorce or loss of one's wife) or a married man instead of a single man or, perhaps most satisfyingly, to a man who is faithful to his wife."

27 R. C. H. Lenski, *The Interpretation of St. Paul's Epistles.*

28 See note 21 above.

29 Grudem, *Systematic Theology*, 917, emphasis in the original.

30 Craig S. Keener, *The IVP Bible Background Commentary: New Testament* (Downers Grove, IL: InterVarsity, 1993), 1 Timothy 3:2-3.

31 Jacob Neusner, *The Mishnah: A New Translation* (New Haven, CT: Yale University Press, 1988), 487.

32 Flavius Josephus and William Whiston, *The Works of Josephus: Complete and Unabridged* (Peabody, MA: Hendrickson, 1987), 120. Antiquities IV, viii.23 (253). Emphasis mine.

33 Professor Heth details the journey of his change of mind, the causes of which he describes as grounded in "conceptual, theological, and exegetical reasons," in his article, "Jesus on Divorce: How My Mind Has Changed," *Southern Baptist Journal of Theology Volume 6* 6, no. 1 (2002): 22. Keener observes how unusual it is for a leading scholar advocating for any particular position to have a change of mind, "I have seen no scholar cited more often than Bill [Heth] in favor of the no-remarriage position, so his reversal (in view of the many who still depend on his former case to prohibit remarriage) is significant... Such reversals are rare among scholars, especially when a scholar has traditionally been hailed as a position's leading defender." Craig Keener, "A Response to William A. Heth" in *Remarriage After Divorce in Today's Church*, ed. Mark L. Strauss and Paul E. Engle, Zondervan Counterpoints Collection (Grand Rapids, MI: Zondervan, 2006), 91. See page 44 in the volume for Heth's rationale for changing his position.

34 William A. Heth, "Remarriage for Adultery or Desertion," in *Remarriage after Divorce in Today's Church*, ed. Mark L. Strauss and Paul E. Engle, Zondervan Counterpoints Collection (Grand Rapids, MI: Zondervan, 2006), 70-71. Underline mine. Italics in the original.

35 Craig S. Keener, *And Marries Another,* 26-27.

36 As Instone-Brewer notes, "The only freedom that makes any sense in this context is the freedom to remarry. We do not have to rely on a process of elimination to decide what this phrase means, because the language that Paul used would have been very plain to any first-century reader. We find similar phraseology in a large number of ancient divorce certificates...all Jewish divorce certificates and most Greco-Roman ones contained the words 'you are free to marry any man you wish,' or something very similar. These words were so important that the rabbis concluded that they were the only words that were essential in a Jewish divorce certificate." David Instone-Brewer. *Divorce*, loc. 2297-2301. See also William A. Heth, "Remarriage," 75. William F. Orr and James Arthur Walther, *I Corinthians: A New Translation, Introduction, With a Study of the Life of Paul, Notes, and Commentary*, 32, *AYB* (New Haven CT; London, England: Yale University Press, 2008),

214, "The deserted partner, then, is free to marry again, whether it be *the brother or the sister.*" Emphasis in original. Joseph A. Fitzmyer, *First Corinthians: A New Translation With Introduction and Commentary*, 32, *AYB* (New Haven, CT; London, England: Yale University Press, 2008), 302. Hans Conzelmann, *1 Corinthians: A Commentary on the First Epistle to the Corinthians*, *Herm.* (Philadelphia, PA: Fortress, 1975), 123. Leon Morris, *1 Corinthians: An Introduction and Commentary*, vol. 7, *Tyndale New Testament Commentaries* (*TNTC*) (Downers Grove, IL: InterVarsity, 1985), 110, "It would be a curious expression to use if Paul meant 'is bound to remain unmarried.'" Alan F. Johnson, *1 Corinthians*, 7, *The IVP New Testament Commentary Series* (*IVPCS*) (Westmont, IL: IVP Academic, 2004), 118. Bruce Winter, "1 Corinthians," in *New Bible Commentary: 21st Century Edition*, ed. D. A. Carson et al., 4th ed. (Downers Grove, IL: InterVarsity, 1994), 1172.

[37] I refer the reader to the detailed analyses of Craig Keener and David Instone-Brewer for a presentation of my basic position on this question. I have some hesitation at some points, especially with Instone-Brewer, but in my estimation both of these treatments accurately present the cultural-historical situation of first century Judaism. See note 32 above for Keener, and note 9 above for Instone-Brewer. For a strong opposing view, I direct the reader to Robert Gagnon's response to David Instone-Brewer here http://www.robgagnon.net/articles/DivorceOUPEntrySexualityS.pdf.

[38] Charles H. Spurgeon, *Lectures to My Students: Complete and Unabridged* (Grand Rapids, MI: Zondervan, 1954), 13-14. Emphasis mine.

[39] See 1 Corinthians 9:27, "But I discipline my body and keep it under control, lest after preaching to others I myself should be disqualified." Also cf. Sirach 37:19, "A man may be shrewd and the teacher of many, and yet be unprofitable to himself" (RSV).

[40] For a helpful guide to the issues of authorship, date, and destination of Ephesians, consult A. Skevington Wood, "Ephesians," *EBC*, 11 (Grand Rapids, MI: Zondervan, 1981), 3-16.

CHAPTER FIVE

Can a Divorced Pastor Lead in Ministry Again?

By Danny Baer, Ph.D.,
retired dean, Southeastern Free Will Baptist College,
Wendell, North Carolina

Is there a way back to ministry for some pastors that involves both forgiveness and accountability?—Doug Carey

When I was a child, growing up in a church in the rural hills of Appalachia, divorce was rare—especially in our churches. In those days there seemed to be no question that not only would a man who had been divorced not be qualified to pastor, but he would *also* not be qualified if his wife had ever been divorced. In fact, divorce was looked upon with such disdain, that church members who had been divorced were restricted in any type of service in the church. The truth was, there were very few divorced people in our neighborhoods. Again, divorce was rare.

Times have changed. Divorce is commonplace in our society and in our churches. A survey by the Barna Group found that one-third of Americans have experienced at least one divorce, and the same survey reported that 26% of evangelicals have done so.[1] Churches have members and workers who have been divorced. Many pastors will now perform weddings of divorced people, and we find divorced men in our pulpits as lead pastors at some of our churches. In a survey of senior pastors, the Barna Group found that 13% had been divorced at least once. (By the way, 83% of these pastors considered themselves as evangelical and 81% as theologically conservative.[2])

How did this happen? It could be that we are victims of the culture we are living in. We are simply trying to cope with the reality of divorce. I remember talking to one pastor who decided to begin marrying couples where at least one partner had been divorced. He said,

I was tired of telling my people, "I have a conviction against marrying anyone who has been divorced. My advice is that you go down the street and have the pastor of that Baptist church marry you. He doesn't have the same conviction. And, by the way, once you are married, make sure you come back and be faithful in my church." It seemed hypocritical.

We can all sympathize with this pastor's moral dilemma. How can we deny performing the marriage of divorcees but be willing to take their tithe? The fact is that most of us have welcomed people who have been divorced into our fellowship. In many churches they can serve in any capacity except become a deacon or a pastor. But is that correct as well? This is a complicated question and the authors of this book have provided perspectives on some of the numerous nuanced aspects of divorce for your consideration. This brings us to the topic of this chapter. Should divorcés be allowed to be ordained? More specifically, if a minister divorces, can he be restored back to the position of lead pastor?

It seems to me there are two extremely important factors at play here: qualification and restoration.

Qualification

And here is where I will take the coward's way out and say that I will not take a position!

Actually, I am not meaning to be cowardly as I am not afraid to state my position. However, stating a position will not settle the issue for everyone. What I would like to do is bring a biblical and contextual perspective that might help all of us take a fresh and honest look at this difficult subject.

Remember, in this chapter we are dealing with the question, *"If a pastor experiences divorce, can he be restored back to the position of lead pastor?"* It is our moral duty under God to try to restore a fallen brother back to a proper relationship with Christ. I hope we can all agree with that. However, does that mean this man, who was once a pastor, is now "qualified" to be a pastor again?

To answer this, we need to step back and ask the broader question, "What qualifies any individual to be a pastor of a church?" To answer this question most people refer to biblical passages, governing treatises or policies, and past practices of the local church or association.

The Bible

The most commonly used Scriptures to ordain ministers so they may be qualified to pastor are 1 Timothy 3 and Titus 1. Both have similar lists of qualifications that are dealt with by the four other authors in this book. Therefore, I will not go into each qualification. I cannot, however, keep from making some pertinent observations and telling a story.

I agree with the author of Chapter Three (Trimble) that ALL the qualifications must be taken into account during the "qualification" process. I remember being a young minister back in those foothills of Appalachia. Our local quarterly association joined with two other associations to form a yearly association. Our local associations would examine men for ordination, but it was the yearly association that handed out our "Minister in Good Standing" cards. These were wallet-sized documents that were given to the ministers to prove they were in good standing with the association for the coming year. To get the card, each minister had to be present at the yearly ministers' meeting and give a report. A long time ago I was a member of a yearly association, as I remember, most of the nearly 100 men would stand up and say something such as "I pastor XYZ Church. I am the husband of one wife, and my wife is the wife of one husband. I have conducted X number of weddings this year and all were qualified to be married." (This meant neither had been divorced.) The man might report other accomplishments and services. After the report the group would vote to give the man his "Minister in Good Standing" card for the coming year. I mention this because in every report the emphasis was on matters related to divorce! Other qualifications were not mentioned such as "I don't drink" or "I am very hospitable." I do not wish to make light of that situation, but there are so many more qualifications than just the one that many believe refers to divorce. I do recall one year, however, that a man stood up and said his teenage son had rebelled against him and he was turning in his card of good standing! Wow! I have always respected that man. By the way, the next year he returned and said his son had gotten right with the Lord and asked for his card back.

I want to talk to all of us who take the strict approach that divorce disqualifies a man in any circumstance. If that is your conviction, I support it. However, I urge you to make sure you are as vehement with all the other qualifications. In fact, I urge all local churches and conferences to carefully study the qualifications in these passages and align the expectations of the ordination process with all qualifications. Credit and background checks are also recommended on any man getting ordained and on any pastoral candidate!

The Denominational Treatise or Polity Manual

Since I have always served in the Free Will Baptist denomination, I will discuss our governing documents. Those of other denominations should consult the treatise, by-laws, or policies your organization.

A Treatise of the Faith and Practices of the National Association of Free Will Baptists, Inc., (Treatise) includes a section on "The Gospel Ministry," which lists the qualifications of ministers. They are brief and read as follows:

> [Ministers] *must possess good, natural and acquired abilities,* [2 Timothy 2:15; 1 Timothy 4:13-15; Titus 1:9; 2:7-8; 2 Timothy 1:7; 2:2; 1 Timothy 3: 2-7]; *deep and ardent piety,* [Psalm 50:16; 2 Timothy 1:8-11, 14; 2:22; 3:5; Titus 1:5-9; 1 Corinthians 2:12-16]; *be especially called of God to the work,* [Acts 20:28; Hebrews 5:4; 1 Corinthians 9:16; Acts 13:2]; *and ordained by prayer and the laying on of hands,* [1 Timothy 4:14; 2 Timothy 1:6; Acts 13:3].[3]

The section referenced above also deals with the duties of ministers, which seems to assume they will serve as pastor along with preaching, visiting, and performing the "work of faithful ministers." In addition, it states that the minister will "administer the ordinances of the Gospel" which is normally part of the pastoral duties.[4]

"The Practices of Free Will Baptists" covers the ordination of ministers. A number of important items are mentioned that are worthy of note.

1. The local church is recognized as the body that has the authority to ordain ministers.
2. In most areas, the authority to ordain ministers has been delegated to the local associations.
3. Ordination is normally preceded by licensing—a period of unspecified length for the minister to prepare for ordination.
4. Some associations will not ordain a minister unless he is involved in a specific ministry.
5. A pastor must at least be licensed, and it is assumed he would soon become ordained.

The Local Church/Association

In Baptistic polity, and in my own denomination, the authority to ordain is in the local church but is often delegated to the district association of which the church is a member. Since our *Treatise* does not deal with the subject (in fact, the word "divorce" does not occur) churches and local associations who ordain men for the work of the ministry must formulate their own guidelines regarding the matter—and they have. A 2020 survey by the Free Will Baptist Committee on Denominational Research found that 23% of our local associations will consider ordaining a divorced man and 55% will ordain a man whose wife has been divorced.[5]

I am reporting practice, not taking a position. The district ordaining council's practice does not equal policy, since each local church and association are self-governing. This decision must be made by each association. This book provides a fresh look at this topic but does not try to dictate to local churches or local associations how they establish their guidelines. This book is not intended to represent denominational policy. I would, however, encourage our pastors on the local level to examine your practices—especially when it comes to the balance of the issue of divorce compared to the other qualifications mentioned in Scripture. The same survey mentioned above found that only 19% of the ordaining committees in our local associations are likely to meet with the wife of the candidate, only 8% run credit checks, and only 5% conduct a criminal background check.

Before I leave the discussion of the local associations and our practice of ordaining men for the ministry, I would like to make an observation that may seem a bit radical. The qualifications found in 1 Timothy and Titus are for the bishop—the overseer. In my opinion, they are not qualifications for a *preacher*, but for a *pastor*. I have often said, "God calls a preacher. A church calls a pastor." Those biblical qualifications are provided as guidelines so the local church may be able to judge the character and qualifications of the man they choose to lead the flock.

And, by inference, the local association or local church can use those same biblical guidelines to know whom to ordain. There is no reason, however, that a person who does not quite fit the qualifications for ordination could not preach the Gospel. Some denominations have "lay preachers" who can be used to fill the pulpit. These individuals need not be ordained, but they could be commissioned and receive similar benefits as ordained ministers—except to pastor, that is. This idea deserves some serious consideration and may allow a divorced man to serve the Lord and fulfill his calling to preach, even though, in most areas, he may never pastor again.

Restoration

Should a man who has been divorced be ordained to preach the Gospel? That is up to the local association and local churches.

Should a pastor who falls be restored by the church? Absolutely! Too many times we tend to "shoot our wounded." It is sad, but there is some truth in this overworked saying. We are quick to say, "Have you heard" rather than shed a tear, speak a prayer, or reach out to a fallen brother who has gone astray.

By the way, this is not optional. Paul wrote, "Brothers and sisters, if someone is caught in sin, you who live by the Spirit should restore that person gently" (Galatians 6:1a, NIV). It is our responsibility to reach out to a fallen brother.

This is personal with me. I grew up with one of the godliest mothers who ever walked this earth. This was not the case with my father. At one point my father took us to church, answered the call to preach, was ordained in the association, and pastored Free Will Baptist churches. However, as I approached my adolescent years my father changed. He turned from pastoring, from church, from God. He turned to worldly entertainment, to drinking, and to other women. My parents did not divorce (although a few years later they separated) but my father had failed. I lived through the heartache of a family who experienced a pastor who fell into sin. I am grateful that I had a pastor, Ed Percell, who loved my dad. I remember him bringing an evangelist to our house to talk to dad one night. At dad's funeral, Pastor Ed said he had gone by the little trailer dad was living in (as a 56-year-old man with wrecked health because of such a sinful life) and he said that dad prayed for God to forgive him. I hang on to the hope that dad did make things right with God.

I did not write this to have you feel sorry for me. I write this to remind all of us that for every preacher we hear has fallen, there are children who are suffering, a wife who is crying herself to sleep and wondering how they are going to survive—and a man who needs someone to reach out to him with the grace of a Savior who still loves him!

The fact is, we do not handle divorce well,[6] especially the divorce of a man whom we have expected to be above reproach. Often, we do not know what to do. We are shocked at the news, angry at the man, saddened for the family, and embarrassed of what others will think. We are quick to point our finger at the idiocy of the dead and slow to lift our fallen brother in prayer. We know that someone needs to do something. However, we may not know what to do.

A few years ago, Free Will Baptists recognized this problem and a Ministerial Family Life Committee was formed. The purpose of the committee was "to develop a ministry of restoration for our leaders."[7]

The recommendations included in the report began with the statement, "The goal of restoration is to bring reconciliation and healing to the individual, his family, and all involved parties; and help the individual to become an established, steadfast Christian, and a worthwhile member of the local church he chooses to attend." The other recommendations centered around the establishment of a committee from "the group responsible for discipline." Presumably, this "group" would frequently be from the local association but could also be formed in the local church.

The Ministerial Family Life Committee continued their work and in 1995 their report to the National Association centered upon prevention and primarily contained two works written by committee members.[8]

There were two sets of procedures prepared that were included in that report. First there was "'Step-By-Step' Procedure for Local Church Disciplinary Action Concerning Its Church Members." The other was, "'Step-By-Step' Procedure in Association Disciplinary Action Concerning Its Ministers."[9]

I applaud the work of the Ministerial Family Life Committee. Their reports, writings, recommendations, and proposed procedures should be read and used by our local churches and associations. However, in their reports, the call for action primarily focused upon what the local church or local association should do. I would like to end this chapter on a more personal note. What can you do? How can you help? What is your moral obligation in reaching out to a brother in Christ who is facing, or who has experienced a failed marriage—no matter the cause? Where is your compassion?

Resources

There are a number of resources available to aid in the restoration of a fallen brother and to aid in prevention. I consulted two men who have doctorates in the field and who have helped countless individuals with their wise and biblical counseling. Dr. Neil Gilliland, director of member care of IM, Inc., recommends Fairhaven Ministries (fairhaven-ministries.net) where he has sent people for any number of issues. Free Will Baptist Executive Secretary, Dr. Eddie Moody, suggested Faithful and True Ministries (faithfulandtrue.com). Dr. Moody has also written a number of books that can be of help, *First Aid: Sexual Issues*, *First Aid: Marriage*, *First Aid for Your Ministry*, and *Ministering in a Changing Sexual Landscape*.

A Personal Note

At this point, I must give a personal testimony. This is not easy for me to write. And, as you read it, you may begin to feel that I am way off track. But stay with me. I have a point that needs to be made.

A few years ago, my wife and I heard news of a close family member who had chosen a lifestyle that was against everything we stood for and believed. I went through the classic stages of grief: shock and denial, bargaining (with the family member and God), anger (at the family member and God), depression (there were times I thought it would be better if I were dead), and, finally, acceptance. I have not accepted this lifestyle. However, I have come to realize that no matter what my family members do and no matter how they act, they are still my own. I came to understand there were often things about my children, or family members, or friends, or acquaintances with which I did not agree. I came to realize it is not my job, nor my obligation to judge them—that my anger toward them is destructive to our relationship and to my own peace of heart. Vindictive words and actions will not help, but will drive a wedge between us and, at best hinder, and at worst ruin any chance to have a relationship with them. And if I lose my relationship, then I miss out on being a spiritual influence or rescuing them. I may ruin my opportunity to lead them to forgiveness and restoration in the arms of a dear and loving Savior.

I get emotional when I think of this—my heart is heavy, I feel a lump in my throat, and I am on the verge of tears. Would to God that I—that all of us—would feel the same compassion for that preacher who has fallen. Let us not forget that David fell into grave sin. And even though the effects of his sin were felt all his life, after his repentance God used David in mighty ways. If God believes in restoration, so should we.

Endnotes ─────────────────────────────────────

[1] The Barna Group (2008). New Marriage and Divorce Statistics Revealed. www.barna.com/research/new-marriage-and-divorce-statistics-released/. See also: Shaunti Feldhahn and Tally Whitehead, The Good News About Marriage: Debunking Discouraging Myths About Marriage and Divorce, (Colorado Springs, CO: Multnomah: 2014). According to the US Census, 71% of Americans are still married to their first spouse. And the 29% that are not still married includes widows. For those who regularly attend church, the divorce rate drops 25–50% below the national average.

[2] The Barna Group (2001). A Profile of Protestant Pastors in Anticipation of "Pastor Appreciation Month," www.barna.com/research/a-profile-protestant-pastors-in-anticipation-of-pastor-appreciation-month/.

[3] A Treatise of the Faith and Practices of the National Association of Free Will Baptists, Inc., The Executive Office NAFWB, Inc. 2013, 14.

[4] Ibid.

[5] Free Will Baptist Committee on Denominational Research. (2020). 2020 Free Will Baptist Ordination Practices Survey. www.nafwb.org/research.

[6] Buxbaum, R. (1995). When Pastors Divorce: A New Approach to Congregational Healing. The Journal of Pastoral Care, 49(2), 173-186. https://doi.org/1.1177/002234099504900207.

[7] Ministerial Family Life Committee (1994). Report of the Ministerial Life Committee. Found in the 1995 Digests of Reports of the National Association of Free Will Baptists.

[8] Ministerial Family Life Committee (1995). Report of the Ministerial Life Committee. Found in the 1995 Digests of Reports of the National Association of Free Will Baptists.

[9] Ministerial Family Life Committee (1999). Report of the Ministerial Life Committee. Found in the 1999 Digests of Reports of the National Association of Free Will Baptists.

A Restored and Rejoicing Pastor

By Doug Carey, pastor,
Crossroads Free Will Baptist Church,
Jenks, Oklahoma

I graduated from Welch College in 1985 and had previously answered God's call to preach and pastor. In my final two years of college, I wondered where the Lord would lead me and who was the future Mrs. Carey. Obviously, I needed a wife to minister—or so I had been taught. I met a lady with a strong Christian background. After months of dating, prayer, and conversation about her willingness to serve in ministry with me, we married just before graduation. Two years later, I accepted the call from a church in Florida as their pastor, my first full-time ministry. Over the next three years, we saw church growth, purchased our first home, and lived the American Dream. What could go wrong?

Almost imperceptibly, my wife became more and more indifferent to the ministry…and to me. During the fall of 1990 my wife changed, practically overnight. We experienced two miscarriages. She changed jobs and began working later and spending time with fellow female co-workers. Within a few weeks, a drastic transformation had taken place in her character, attitude, and even in how she dressed. I felt powerless.

She soon informed me that she no longer loved me, wanted no opportunity for reconciliation, and moved out just before Christmas. I took a trip over Christmas, too, back to my hometown, of Blanchester,

Ohio. I landed in Cincinnati, rented a car, and I drove to the cemetery where my parents were buried. Overcome by shame and burdened by failure, I knelt at my parents' graves and wept.

With absolute certainty she would not change her mind, two weeks later, through tears, I resigned as pastor, attempting to explain the gut-wrenching pain of loss to my church. None of us can control another person's free will. We can pray, pressure, cajole, and try to convince. But in the end, she would not be dissuaded. My marriage, my ministry—and career calling—was over.

It was difficult finding employment as obviously there was not a great demand in central Florida for former ministers with theology degrees. I was alone and adrift in emotional discouragement. In fact, I well remember thinking how easily a seriously depressed person who had experienced such a devastating blow could consider suicide. Thankfully, my confidence in God, and His continued reassurance in my life protected me from such thoughts. I *knew* God was still at my side. He was *still* leading…even if I did not know where or how.

I remained in church and faithful to the Lord. I taught Sunday School, filled in for pastors on vacation, and decided the Lord was leading me back to Nashville to start over. My good friend, Rob Morgan, had offered me the position of *Singles Again* leader at the Donelson Fellowship. I jumped at the opportunity to feel useful in ministry again, even if it was merely a volunteer position.

Starting over was not as easy as I hoped it would be. Surrounded by successful pastors and professors (some of whom I had attended college with ten years earlier), I felt like a second-class believer. I was not treated in such a manner—the earlier feelings of failure, shame, and spiritual inadequacy had returned and were all mine. But slowly, God began to repair my brokenness. It was good to be in a familiar church again, good to be with *my* people again. While volunteering in the singles ministry, I met a young lady who had graduated from Randall University. Lorrie Sutterfield, a tremendous vocalist, had moved to Nashville.

God brought her from Oklahoma one month before he brought me from Florida, and to the same church. We do not serve a God of coincidence!

We began dating during the summer of 1992, and took our time, praying and seeking God's will during the following months. We were married in the spring of 1993 at her home church in Norman, Oklahoma, and spent a wonderful first year together volunteering in our Nashville church, teaching our own Sunday School class, and enjoying life.

Nearly a year after our marriage, God began moving in my heart and spirit concerning returning to pastoral ministry. We prayed much, talked much, and I sought counsel from leaders within our denomination. Some said, "Doug, I am sorry for what happened to you…and it's not your fault, but you simply cannot lead a church again. You're disqualified." Others advised me to seek out another denomination because "Free Will Baptists would never give you another chance." Yet more than a few plainly stated, "Doug, do what God calls you to do, regardless of what others think. If you do that, then God will lead and restore you."

I valued our heritage, our doctrine, our family. A small church in Mobile, Alabama, expressed interest in me. Having been completely honest and forthright about my past—and providing personal references from the leaders of my church in Florida—they voted to call me as pastor in May 1994. Since those days, I have led two other Free Will Baptist Churches to long-lasting spiritual, numerical, and financial growth. I presently serve as the moderator of our local association, served on the state Christian education board, and the executive board of my previous association. Lorrie and I have been married since 1993 and have enjoyed God's rich blessings on our family and marriage. It truly has been a miraculous journey from those dark days in the Sunshine State 31 years ago.

If you are a hurting minister, I trust you find a measure of comfort and edification. Indeed, I have spoken to many former pastors through the years who felt similar abandonment; pastors who to this day still hurt and are still looking for a place to serve. My prayer is this book encourages hurting ministers, informs ordaining councils, and perhaps redeems some ministries that are worthy of restoration.